Twayne's United States Authors Series

Sylvia E. Bowman, *Editor*

INDIANA UNIVERSITY

Edwin Arlington Robinson

(TUSAS) 137

EDWIN ARLINGTON ROBINSON

By HOYT C. FRANCHERE

Portland State College

TWAYNE PUBLISHERS
A DIVISION OF G. K. HALL & CO., BOSTON

Contents

Preface

TODAY, any student who would study the life and work of Edwin Arlington Robinson must follow a well-worn path. He will begin with the brief but important memoir of Mrs. Laura Richards, *E. A. R.*, for Mrs. Richards was a lifelong friend and correspondent of the Maine poet. He will read the Hagedorn biography and the Robinson study by Emery Neff. He will turn next, perhaps, to Edwin Fussell's examination of Robinson's background as a traditional poet. He will examine the critical evaluations of Robinson's work by Yvor Winters and by the French critic, Charles Cestre. He will become absorbed in the thorough and carefully ordered critical approach to Robinson's poetry made by Ellsworth Barnard, whose position is both knowledgeable and sane and whose style is felicitously unencumbered by critical cant. Finally, he will read carefully the early letters that Robinson wrote to Harry DeForest Smith, edited by Dunham Sutcliffe and, more recently published, the memoir of Chard Powers Smith, *Where the Light Falls*. If he has the time, the student will read whatever other of Robinson's letters he can find, as well as a large package of scholarly articles, dissertations, pamphlets, and books on the poet's accomplishments.

I cannot apologize for following the plainly marked trail to Robinson's door. Robinson has been the subject of more speculation, I think, than almost any other poet of our time. His native reticence and modesty, his propensity for understatement, and his frequent lapses into introspection and self-critical analysis as they are found in his letters have created only half an image of the real man. His poems, so many of his critics insist, reveal him as a dark mind dwelling on darker subjects. Some of these views need to be clarified, others refuted.

However, my intent in this brief document is not to re-establish Robinson's stature on the literary scene, for he has really never lost it. To be sure, his reputation suffered a decline during the decade after his death in 1935; but the poet is, in the 1960's, reclaiming his deservedly high rank among American poets. I have therefore tried, first of all, to discover what in Robinson's life—his associations, the books he read, the letters he wrote, the work he failed to do or succeeded in doing—most significantly influenced and shaped his mind. Second, I have attempted to sift through his poetic canon in order to recognize his most often repeated symbols and their meanings and to discover those themes that most often pervade his poems, both short and long. Inevitably, as I have sifted the vast body of his work I have been compelled to exclude from consideration a great number of his poems. For one thing, a work of this nature demands selectivity. For another, some of the later and longer poems (*Avon's Harvest, Dionysus in Doubt,* or *On the Way,* for example) are unrewarding subjects for close analysis; and they contribute little to Robinson's reputation as a poet.

And finally, I have found it needful to set the usually accepted story of Robinson's long career in contrast to the little known and, until recently, unpublished account of what I have called "the Robinson myth" as I have learned of its essential details; but I do not use the term "myth" as an archetypal (that is, as a Jungian or unconscious) pattern but rather as a kind of design that hovers between the imagined and the real in Robinson's poetry. Always acknowledging the insubstantial, even tenuous, nature of the intimate family relationships connected with this myth, I yet have found the study helpfully revealing. It is basic to an analysis of some of the poems and to a recognition of the underlying thematic development in a large part of Robinson's poetry. But I have, I hope, put the myth into its proper perspective.

In the making of this book I have leaned inescapably and gratefully upon those who have preceded me in their studies of Robinson. Since I began my reading of his poetry nearly forty years ago, I cannot now say just which critic enlightened me most about which poem. Those whose ideas I have been able specifically to identify I have of course properly acknowledged. What follows will,. I trust, give the student another view of Robinson and a further appreciation and understanding of his poetic achievement.

HOYT C. FRANCHERE

Portland State College

Acknowledgments

For permission to quote from many of Robinson's poems I wish to thank the Macmillan Company. From the 1946 edition of *Collected Poems* I have reproduced fragments of the following: "Captain Craig," "The Cameron Men," "Late Summer," "The Book of Annandale," "Mortmain," "Bokardo," "Flammonde," "Aunt Imogen," "Isaac and Archibald," "The Sheaves," "Merlin," "Tristram," "The Growth of 'Lorraine,'" "The Man Who Died Twice," "Amaranth," "John Gorham," "Eros Turranos," "Cavender's House," "Matthias at the Door," "Ben Jonson Entertains a Man from Stratford," and "King Jasper."

To Charles Scribner's Sons I am also indebted for permission to reproduce entirely or in part the following of Robinson's poems: "George Crabbe," "Octaves," and "Her Eyes," from *The Children of the Night* (1910); "Exit," and "Two Gardens of Linndale," from *The Town Down the River* (1910).

It is pleasant to record the courteous reception that I had at the Colby College Library, the Houghton Library, the Williams College Library, and the New York Public Library, where Robinson collections are domiciled. I am grateful to these libraries for permission occasionally to quote small portions of letters that are in their possession. To the Harvard University Press I owe my thanks for permission to quote fragments of letters printed in *Untriangulated Stars: Letters of Edwin Arlington Robinson to Harry DeForest Smith*. From other libraries and private collections—notably the collection of Mr. C. Waller Barrett—I was generously offered copies of Robinson letters for whatever use I might make of them.

Above all, I am grateful to Robinson's niece, Mrs. William Nivison, and to her son, David Nivison, Associate Professor of Philosophy at Stanford University. Both received me graciously and gave me invaluable help, not only with the information that they offered concerning Robinson's life and work but also with their comment and criticism on some parts of this book. Of particular significance was the opportunity that they gave me to read an unpublished *Memoir* written about EAR by one member of the family. I am further indebted to Mrs. Nivison for permission to reprint the Bradford Perin sketch of Robinson that is now domiciled in the Williams College Library.

I am happy also to record the dedicated assistance of Mr. Edmond Gnoza, Librarian of the Division of Arts and Letters at Portland State College; for he has become veritably a partner in all by searches for library and museum materials. And I wish to make special note of my thanks to my friends and colleagues at Portland State College, Mrs. Alvin Nelson, Assistant Professor of English, and Egbert Oliver and Samuel Yorks, Professors of English, for their willingness to read my manuscript and to give me many helpful suggestions for revision.

Finally, I join the ranks of the many who have written books for TUSAS and who are, like me, forever grateful to our patient and understanding, as well as perceptive, editor, Professor Sylvia Bowman.

Chronology

1869   Edwin Arlington Robinson born, December 22, at Head Tide, Maine, the third son (following Dean and Herman) of Edward and Mary Palmer Robinson.

1870   Family moved to Gardiner, Maine, in September.

1885   Probably at this time first came under the wing of Alanson Tucker Schumann, who brought him into the "Club," a small group of local poets who wrote and read poetry at their meetings.

1888-   Graduated from Gardiner High School. Spent a post-
1889   graduate year studying Horace and Milton.

1891-   Entered Harvard as a "special" student; published poems
1893   in *The Harvard Advocate.*

1892   Father died.

1893   Family in serious financial difficulties, owing to bad investments in Western real estate.

1893-   In Gardiner, wrote poetry; tried unsuccessfully to write
1896   and sell short stories. With Harry DeForest Smith, translated Sophocles' *Antigone.*

1896   Had printed at his own expense *The Torrent and the Night Before* (Cambridge, the Riverside Press). Mother died of "black diphtheria."

1897   Spent a short time in New York. *The Children of the Night.*

1899   Served on President Eliot's administrative staff at Harvard from January to June. Returned to New York. Dean Robinson died in September.

1902   The manuscript of *Captain Craig,* lost for a time by Small, Maynard and Company editor, finally published by Houghton, Mifflin Company.

1903-   Employed as a time-checker during the construction of
1904   New York's first subway.

1905-   Through his son, Kermit, Theodore Roosevelt read *The*
1909   *Children of the Night,* was impressed by it, and wrote a critical estimate of the poetry in *The Outlook;* he appointed Robinson to a position in the New York office of the Collector of Customs, a sinecure that the poet held

until he resigned, June, 1909. Attempted unsuccessfully to write plays for the New York stage: *Van Zorn* and *The Porcupine*. Herman Robinson died.

1911   Spent the first of twenty-four summers at the MacDowell Colony, Peterborough, New Hampshire.

1914   *Van Zorn* published by Macmillan.

1915   *Captain Craig* reprinted.

1916   *The Man Against the Sky.*

1917   *Merlin.* From 1917 until 1922, received a gift of money from anonymous donors.

1919   In his fiftieth year honored by tributes of his contemporaries in *The New York Times Book Review*.

1920   *Lancelot; The Three Taverns.*

1921   *Avon's Harvest.* His *Collected Poems* awarded the Pulitzer Prize.

1923   *Roman Bartholow.* Visited England, April-July.

1924   *The Man Who Died Twice.* Received his second Pulitzer Prize.

1925   *Dionysus in Doubt.*

1927   *Tristram* a brillant success. Third award of the Pulitzer Prize.

1929-   *Cavender's House; The Glory of the Nightingales; Selec-*
1934   *ted Poems; Matthias at the Door; Nicodemus; Talifer; Amaranth.*

1935   Died, April 6, in New York Hospital. *King Jasper,* published posthumously.

CHAPTER 1

My Father Was to Me
a Mighty Stranger

O N DECEMBER 22, 1869, Edwin Arlington Robinson was
born in his father's home beside the Sheepscot River in
Head Tide, Maine; but he was not to remain long in this quiet
hamlet. For though the father, Edward Robinson, had accumulated something of a fortune, buying and selling timber and
keeping store, he decided to move his family to the thriving
town of Gardiner, only a few miles away. Edwin was to write
about Head Tide to his sister-in-law many years later: ". . . I
don't remember it very well, having lived in it only six months.
I didn't walk about the town to any great extent and so never
got well acquainted with my neighbors."[1]

It is Gardiner that justly claims Edwin Arlington Robinson
as a native son. There where the power-producing Cobbossee
River bounds into the Kennebec (at that time a river which
ocean-going ships plied regularly), paper, lumber, and textile
mills had already made a prosperous way of life for the leading
townspeople when Edward Robinson moved his family in 1870 so
that his sons might have the advantages of a good education.
Investing in local businesses and banks, the father soon became
recognized as a man of substance, destined to take a significant
place in the life of the community.

As for the poet's lineage, if fact and legend have been sifted
carefully—and most of Robinson's friends and friendly bio-
graphers have examined the record—there was at least one
Robinson family in Head Tide, or downstream on the Sheepscot,
a generation or two before Edwin Robinson appeared.[2] The
poet's mother, Mary Palmer Robinson, descended from Thomas
Dudley, one time Lieutenant-Governor of the Massachusetts Bay

Colony. One of Dudley's daughters, Anne, married Simon Bradstreet, and became one of the earliest of American poets. The other, Mercy, married John Woodbridge, directly Robinson's ancestor on his mother's side. Although his family may not have been illustrious New England folk, it was yet distinguished by the names of some people of stature and competence; and it was tested and strengthened by the often unfriendly and rigorous conditions of life thrust upon Maine's pioneers and their descendants.

I   A Different Boy

A neighbor of the Robinson family once described the poet's father as a big and powerful man, an incongruous and marked contrast to his younger, somewhat delicate and refined wife.[3] But, for all the incongruity of their natures, no matter how their differences of character may have shaped the lives of their three sons, Edward and Mary Robinson were apparently a devoted pair and, to the end, dependent upon each other. In the big house on Lincoln, high above the Kennebec, father, mother, and the three boys lived a comfortable existence. Dean, the eldest son, was given more to books than to vigorous physical activity; the father regarded him as best suited to the medical profession. Herman, eight years younger than Dean, was exceptionally good to look at, easily won friends, and became popularly regarded as the logical successor to his father in a business career. Four years younger still, Edwin found no companionship with his brothers, sought playmates just across the street in Captain Jordan's home, and there heard tales of great adventures on the vast expanses of the oceans.

But his childhood friendships were not limited to the Jordans, favorites though they were. The names of Atwood, Longfellow, Swanton, and Morrell were among those he came to know in the primary school of Mrs. Morrell, not far from the two-acre playground of his own back yard. As a companion, too, he had a rocking chair in which, insignificantly dwarfed, he rocked and read and reflected upon the misfortune of his ever having been born. At six he could quote from Campbell's "Lochiel's Warning"; and the now thrice-told, though never confirmed, story of his reading Poe's "Raven" to his mother while sitting on her kitchen floor marks his early interest in poetry. Were this latter poem not morbid enough for him, young Edwin found grimmer reading in the medical books of his brother Dean, wherein he discovered portraits of the human figure in varying stages of deterioration, rotted by such hideous diseases as leprosy and elephantiasis and falling of the womb. Pondering these, as well as life and death as he witnessed the solemn processions moving slowly into a neighboring cemetery, made of this dark-eyed, sensitive man-child a frightened hypochondriac. A thousand times he may have pictured himself half eaten through and chilled and already ripe for the graveyard beyond his father's home. He asked himself how soon he would follow to the grave his close friend, Harry Morrell, who was a victim of diphtheria at eleven years of age.

As he grew older, however, "Win," as Robinson was called by his primary school playmates, escaped from these terrors into games and laughter, and into the even more fascinating enterprises of collecting bugs and words. Sprouting into a tall, angular, and ill-coordinated boyhood, he swam with the other lads in the Kennebec River, built rafts, and in the winter slid down the plunging Gardiner hills or skated on the frozen river, on the ponds of ice that formed quickly behind the ice cutters. But apart from coasting on Herman's sled that he was heir to, he developed no great skill in any of the outdoor sports.

Although he was always readily accepted by his fellows and although he persistently met every physical challenge, he appeared to tire more easily than the others, as is often the case with youngsters who grow too fast. At night his ankles and legs ached from his exertions.

Some years later, Win told his sister-in-law, Herman's wife, that at that time he regarded himself as different from the other boys: not queer, but not quite fitting the general pattern. Such an attitude is surely not uncommon among the supersensitive. Dean, gifted and intelligent, was at twenty-two on his way to what all believed would be a highly successful career in medicine. Herman, handsome, outgoing, and always popular, unavoidably kept his younger brother in the shadow. The father's attention, at any rate, appears to have been devoted chiefly to Dean and Herman; it was almost as if Win had been an unplanned and unexpected child and, therefore, usually ignored. Win Robinson doubtless experienced moments of self-pity and feelings of insecurity and rejection that darkened his world from time to time. But it would be a serious mistake to look upon him as forever blighted, as the victim and the prophet of doomsday.

However, he welcomed the respite a storm would bring him —winter or summer—and the comfortable solitude of books. For a time, with another boy or two he hunted and collected insects and early learned, in his perspicuous and quiet way, that (as he was to write years afterward in his "Ben Jonson") "It's all a world where bugs and emperors / Go singularly back to the same dust, / Each in his time." Early, too, he established a life-long preoccupation with words; and in a completely unscientific manner he sought and collected and locked them in his memory where they would await his need. Even at ten he played word games with Gus and Alice Jordan, each trying to outdo the other in finding the longest ones, such as Melchizedek and Nebuchad-nezzar.

Many years later he was to write that he became "an in-corrigible fisher of words who thought nothing of fishing for two weeks to catch a stanza, or even a line, that he would not throw back into a squirming sea of language where there was every word but the one he wanted. . . ."⁴ One would find him, years later, rocking in a chair in one of his numerous rented "rooms" in New York or in the home of Louis LeDoux at Corn-wall-on-Hudson, at Peterborough in his studio, or at Mrs. Perry's in Boston: forever rocking and searching for words and weaving their magic into the fabric of his poetry.

How much does a boy of ten read? And what takes his fancy? Edward Robinson's *Ex Libris* appears in a copy of Bryant's *Library of Poetry and Song* found in his son's collection of books. There can be no question that the youngest Robinson grew familiar with lines of both English and American poets whose work appears in that volume. But as he was to write Mrs. Richards in 1929, when he was young he read "mostly Dickens, Dime Novels (which cost five cents), Elijah Kellogg, Harry Castleman, Oliver Optic, Horatio Alger, Bulwer-Lytton, Thacke-ray. . . ."⁵ All his life he turned to mysteries and to adventure stories, doubtless as an anodyne or as company to him in lonely, insomniac hours. But the reading habit, begun early, was never to leave him; he read voluminously.

At the age of eleven he made probably his first attempts at verse, though these have disappeared. Mrs. Richards wrote that one day at school Win found some classmates in the cellar, pulled a sheaf of verses from his pocket, and read them to an unappreciative audience. Discouraged by their rejection, he tossed his treasure into the furnace; and, as Mrs. Richards says, "we have no juvenilia." Meanwhile, he finished his elementary grades; and in 1883, shortly before his fourteenth birthday, he entered Gardiner High School to take the scientific rather than the Classical, college-preparatory course. Although a few colleges and universities were then revolting from the tradition of the classics requirement for entrance, the revolt was by no means universal; and, by following the more practical curriculum, Win Robinson necessarily gave up, for the time being, whatever plans he may have entertained for a college education.

To a great extent Edward Robinson was responsible for Edwin's choice of the scientific course. The father was not only indifferent about his youngest son but about his education, for the young Edwin explained in a letter to his close friend, Arthur Gledhill: "No, Art, I have entirely given up all ideas of going to college. . . . If I had not made the mistake that I did in supposing that it would be impossible for me to take a college course on account of 'home rule' things would have probably turned out in a different manner. Father always talked down colleges and claimed they did more harm than good; and consequently when I entered high school I never gave the thing a thought. It was not until I entered the first class that I began to consider the question seriously and I am afraid the fact is that I had not the *sand* to turn back the leaves . . . and prepare myself."[6] Not long afterward, however, he wrote Gledhill in quite another vein: "Three weeks ago today I spent the Sunday with Smith [Harry DeForest Smith] at Bowdoin. It was a new thing to me and awoke all my latent desire for a taste of college life. For the past two or three months I have been harboring an idea that I may take a year's course next fall in something (I have not decided what) at Harvard. You may remember that I was 'contemplating' three years ago."[7]

Perhaps had Edwin insisted or pleaded, he might have secured his father's permission to take the classical course in high school. But a boy of thirteen does not always know what he wants to do, nor were there urgent social pressures in Gardiner persuading him to look forward to a college education. What is chiefly revealed in his letters to Gledhill is that he was not one then—and was never to become one—to drive or push others in order to achieve his personal desires or wishes.

Several years before he contemplated taking courses at Harvard as a "special" student, however, Win Robinson made the acquaintance of Alanson Tucker Schumann, a neighbor and a practitioner of homeopathic medicine in Gardiner. Schumann, himself a graduate of Gardiner High School, had studied homeopathy in New York and had then returned to practice in his home town.[8] Once settled there, he began writing poetry, probably about 1876. There can be little doubt that the influence of his high school teacher, Miss Caroline Swan, had first turned him to verse writing; in any case, he associated with her and with Judge Henry Sewell Webster, both of whom dabbled with poetry. For several years the three met weekly for an evening of poetry reading and critical comment.

Win Robinson knew, of course, about Schumann's avocational interest. He was indeed a shy lad, but he somehow found the courage one day to tuck a sheaf of poems under his arm and to knock at Schumann's door. Details of this memorable meeting cannot be found, if in fact they ever existed in written form; but something in young Robinson appealed to Schumann. Twenty-three years the poet's elder, he nevertheless developed a sincere interest in Edwin, encouraged him, tutored him in the poetic art, took Robinson to meetings of his poetry "Club," and introduced him to the gentle Judge Webster and to the High Priestess, Miss Swan. The latter, ancient as she was in 1937, recalled Win's appearances at these meetings, noting that the young poet was a very determined young man,[9] and that, while Schumann was certainly Robinson's teacher, *she*, after all, had taught Schumann. However, Schumann's tutelage was confined to poetry—of this much Miss Swan was certain. In his study of the relationship between Robinson and the homeopath, Peter Deckert points out that the younger man must have frowned upon the doctor's propensity for skirt-chasing and, it may have been, his swigging, too.[10] Schumann could easily have served as prototype for Robinson's John Evereldown. Yet man and boy shared a strong kinship in poetry, one influencing the other even though inevitably Win Robinson was the poet and Schumann the maker of verses that never, or almost never, were better than "minor songs."

Robinson wrote an unenthusiastic obituary on Schumann when the doctor died in 1918. Twelve years later, for whatever reason he may have had to change his views, he spoke in quite another vein. Recalling his youthful preoccupation with poetry, he wrote:

> I was chiefly occupied with the composition of short poems and sonnets, which I would read to my old friend and neighbor, Dr. A. T. Schumann, who was himself a prolific writer of sonnets, ballades and rondeaus, and a master of poetic technique. As I shall never know the extent of my indebtedness to his interest and belief in my work, or to my unconscious absorption of his technical enthusiasm, I am glad for this obvious opportunity to acknowledge a debt that I cannot even estimate . . . [He] told me once that I should have to write poetry or starve, and that I might do both—although he did not believe that I should starve, or not exactly. That was encouraging, and I have never forgotten it . . . . [As] it was, I am sure, that [*sic*] he was one of the most remarkable metrical technicians that ever lived, and an invaluable friend to me in those years of apprenticeship when time, as a commodity to be measured and respected, did not exist.[11]

Here Robinson expressed what must have been the simple truth: "I shall never know the extent of my indebtedness to his [Schumann's] interest and belief in my work." The two obviously shared a mutual enthusiasm for and an understanding of the poets whose work they read. Thus in 1894, Robinson wrote Harry DeForest Smith that he found "infinite pleasure" in Cowper's *The Task*.[12] He was equally pleased and moved by George Crabbe, and in one of his early sonnets said of him

> Whether or not we read him, we can feel
> From time to time the vigor of his name
> Against us like a finger for the shame
> And emptiness of what our souls reveal
> In books that are as altars when we kneel
> To consecrate the flicker, not the flame.[13]

Schumann had himself written a group of seven sonnets, all about Crabbe; and one of these reads, in part:

> Some power occult impelled his pen to move
> In zeal unwearied on the waiting page:
> His poet-labor was his choicest love—
> His life-work by its purity we gage [*sic*]:
> Of stirring verse he gave the world enough
> To shame the rhymsters of the present age.[14]

Schumann's verse seems undeniably to indicate a parallel development of ideas in Robinson that also may be found in other of their mutual interests.[15]

But Schumann was not all of Robinson's life in these forming and informing years. During the high school days and after, for a time, Win Robinson found such friends as Harry Smith, Art Gledhill, and Ed Moore altogether congenial and uncritical of his ambition to write poetry. Smith graduated a year ahead of the others and went on with his own ambition to study the classics at Bowdoin. Robinson, Gledhill, and Moore—spending an extra year in high school when the school board bowed to the wish of the principal to raise the standards at Gardiner High by adding a year to the course of study—formed a League of Three, were given such special privileges as independent study in the school belfry, and learned the delights of pipes and chewing tobacco. Robinson had already translated into blank verse the entire oration of Cicero against Cataline, and in this last of his high school years he was to find his way through Virgil. He went on to graduate in the class of 1888, recognized as one of the leaders and sharing (along with Gledhill, who delivered an address in Greek) a part in the commencement exercises by writing and reading the class poem. These were, indeed, the happiest moments of Win Robinson's early life.

II   *Vagaries of Life*

At home, however, not all was well—and was never to be well, or so it seems now. Edwin's oldest brother, Dean, having overexposed himself to the severe winters of coastal Maine during his fledgling years as a general practitioner, has been victimized first by acute neuralgia and then by morphine, which he took to ease the pain. Even before Win graduated, Dean had returned an addict to his father's hearth, seldom again to practice. Edward Robinson handed his business interests over to his handsome and energetic son Herman and withdrew into an inactive retirement. Mary Palmer Robinson uncomplainingly catered to his needs and continued to manage the household. Confidently, Herman persuaded his father to liquidate his Maine holdings and to invest in Western properties, a shift that seemed to promise substantial profits but that ultimately meant devastating losses for the family; for no one then could have anticipated the collapse in the American economy that came in the early 1890's. During this period, Win fell heir to Herman's chores about the house while Herman engaged the wide-eyed notice of the young ladies in Gardiner.

Precisely how the youngest Robinson responded to the vagaries in his family's life at this time can only be guessed since he did not often write about things domestic in his letters— or, if he did so, the letters are not presently available to the searcher. With some regularity he continued to meet with Doctor Schumann and the other members of the "Club" who, under Miss Swan's guidance, were studying French forms of poetry—forms with which Robinson was soon experimenting. His "Ballade of Broken Flutes," addressed to Schumann, his "Villanelle of Change," and the favorite "House on the Hill" reflect this early preoccupation with French metrical patterns.

But the year wrought changes in Robinson's outlook. The League of Three was now a thing of the past, never, the young poet lamented, to be renewed. Early in 1889 Win learned that Art Gledhill was planning to be married. On February 23, he wrote his friend: "It's all right, old man; go ahead. I think I have mentioned to Gus, before I received this epistle, something to the effect that your affections were captured . . . but you need not be alarmed by the fear that I shall break the confidence you have placed in me."[16] Robinson was, however, clearly unprepared to face the reality of a "loss" of his friend. Friendships meant then, and were always to mean, a great deal more to him than they perhaps mean to most men in our age; repeatedly, when writing to Gledhill or to Smith in the next few years, he revealed his nostalgia for their friendship and companionship. The year brought other losses, too, of greater significance and of far more devastating consequences. This period also raised issues within the family circle that were not to be resolved for many years; and, as we shall see in a later chapter, they directly concerned Robinson's poetry.

At the moment, however, the full force of his loss of close friends did not apparently strike Robinson. ". . . I am keeping time for the Oakland Ice Co and my time is pretty well taken up," he wrote Gledhill. "I have had the very devil of a cough for the past week and I assure you that it has been no pleasant affair to get up at 5:00 and go down on the river to shiver all day. . . . Trusting that Shakespeare's aphorism 'The course of true love, etc.' will be contradicted in your case, I remain the same old anchorite."[17] By November of the same year he was making a poetical translation of Virgil's Third Eclogue, a copy of which he later sent to Gledhill. In a gayer, more facetious mood, he commented: "I am afraid, Art, that I shall have to advertise in the Police Gazette when I yearn towards matrimony. How would this do? A young man of fine character and unquestionable ability having wearied of his hitherto celibate life has decided to appeal to the affections of the gentler sex through the columns of this periodical. The person in question must be blessed with a liberal education, have dark hair and eyes, weigh from 110 to 125 and keep her finger nails clean. She must be of an amiable disposition and not too fond of soused tripe. . . . Think that would fetch one, Art?"[18]

Moments of such levity, though rare enough in the early letters, belie the too commonly held view that Robinson forever "gloomed and mumbled like a soul from Tophet." But his postgraduate year in high school and the following year matured him significantly and brought to him a measure of seriousness that inevitably deepened. They brought periods of doubt and uncertainty and insecurity as well—a prelude to more bitter days, even years, to come. By mid-summer, 1890, he wrote Gledhill that though he had no particular complaints, he found his life a dull one. Dean was weighing ice in Smithtown, and he himself was left alone with his mother to take care of the "farm" and look after his father. Sometimes, he said, a week or ten days went by without his seeing one of the boys in Gardiner. He looked upon himself as a "drone, with no particular opening for the future."[19] He was, he felt, living by himself with a father who by now could scarcely walk a step without his help. And he no longer enjoyed the consolation of chewing tobacco!

By September, as he noted to both Gledhill and Smith, he had a job with Danforth, an engineer; and, as a consequence, he looked forward to joining a river-survey group for a month and to earning fifty dollars. He would have preferred to smoke "a pipe under a tree in August and read Virgil," but he felt driven to earn some money: "Dollars are convenient things to have, De Smith, but this diabolical, dirty race that men are running after them disgusts me. I shall probably outgrow this idea, but until I do I shall labor quite contented under the delusion that [there] is something to life outside of 'business.' Business be damned."[20] Miniver scorned the gold he sought but was annoyed without it! He would have preferred even more ancient things than a pipe under the pines. He heard the voice of Achilles and Aeneas and Priam; he loved the medieval grace of those who lived in his often-read chronicle of wasted time, the names of knights and ladies that, years later, he celebrated in his own songs.

Yet he did not limit his readings to the classics. More and more during the two years before he entered Harvard, he wrote to Smith and Gledhill of books that had struck his fancy, commenting critically upon them in his youthful but sometimes perceptive way. Not all that he picked up to read were poetic works. Such minor novels as Edna Lyall's *Donovan* and *We Two*, for example, Gledhill had suggested to him. He plunged into Thomas Hardy's *The Hand of Ethelberta, Far From the Madding Crowd,* and *Under the Greenwood Tree,* finding in the latter two a "marvelous mixture of pastoral humor and pathos." He went on to *Desperate Remedies, The Mayor of Casterbridge, The Return of the Native,* and *A Pair of Blue Eyes;* and he concluded that Hardy was a greater writer than William Black, whose *Macleod of Dare* he regarded as a great novel, even though Hardy lacked Black's naturalness. He thought Tolstoy's *Kreutzer Sonata* contained too much of the "low-necked truth" to be entrusted to tender youth; and he was unimpressed by Marie Bashkirtseff's *Journal,* which was translated into English in 1890.

Robinson read Frank R. Stockton's *House of Martha* that ran as a serial in *The Atlantic Monthly.* He found Kipling's *The Light that Failed* attractive in a queer way, but thought Kipling's poetry much superior to his prose. He rated Bret Harte's "Outcasts of Poker Flat" as in some ways the "best short story in the English language," a critical judgment that he doubtless qualified in later years. He had already found time for Dickens and Thackeray ("We poor ungifted devils of the common herd know little of the bull-dog persistency and enthusiasm required to bring forth a thing like the *Newcomes* or *Our Mutual Friend*"[21]).

He soaked himself in the "fiery philosophy" of Carlyle's *Sartor Resartus,* which he recommended to Smith as "just the book" for one who is in the midst of "philosophical and psychological moonings." He read and noted in Carlyle's introduction, however, what a "doleful experience" the Scot had had in finding a publisher. "This seems to be the case with nearly all great literary efforts," he wrote, as if divining his own frustrations in the market place. To these books he added such unexpected explorations as those he made into Charles Dudley Warner's *My Summer in a Garden* and Wilkie Collins' *Heart and Science,* thereby illustrating the diversity as well as the undisciplined nature of his reading in these post-graduate years. Nor did he neglect poetry, for he mentions Byron, Keats, Clough, and Omar Khayyam (in FitzGerald's translation).

How much he learned in this long period of largely indiscriminate reading can only be conjectured, but it seems altogether likely that he had formulated the basic frame and concept of poetry. Certain statements made by Bryant in his introduction to *The Family Library of Poetry and Song* that young Win Robinson found on his father's shelves apparently left their mark upon his mind. "To me," Bryant commented,

> it seems that one of the most important requisites for a great poet is a luminous style. The elements of poetry lie in natural objects, in the vicissitudes of human life, in the emotions of the human heart, and the relations of man to man. He who can present them in combinations and lights which at once affect the mind with a deep sense of their truth and beauty is the poet for his own age and the ages that succeed it. It is no disparagement to his skill or his power that he finds them near at hand; the nearer they lie to the common track of the human intelligence, the more certain is he of the sympathy of his own generation, and of those which shall come after him . . .[22]

Some of Robinson's early work reflects his preoccupation with Bryant's critical stipulations, but that he interpreted Bryant according to his own views goes without question. Even as his first collection of poems was readied in 1896, Robinson wrote Gledhill, to whom he sent a copy:

> You won't find much in the book to interest you, but considering you know the man who did it, you may like to look it over. You won't find much in the way of natural description. There is very little tinkling water, and there is not a red-bellied robin in the whole collection. When it comes to "nightingales and roses," I am not "in it," nor have I the smallest desire to be. I sing, in my own particular manner, of heaven and hell and now and then

of material things (supposing they exist) of a more prosy con-
notation than those generally admitted into the domain of metre.
In short I write whatever I think is appropriate to the subject
and let tradition go to the deuce.[23]

There are, to be sure, no red-bellied robins and no tinkling
water in Robinson's poetry, but he had much to say of the vicissitudes of human life, of the emotions of the human heart, and of
the relations of man to man—and his poetry was couched in
words that assuredly did not belong to the poetic guild of his
own era. Moreover, he found the subjects of his poems near at
hand and close to the common track of the human intelligence.
And though these poems reflect his individual variants of Bryant's
precepts, they nonetheless indicate his indebtedness to Bryant
just as, quite clearly, they reflect his admitted indebtedness to
Alanson Tucker Schumann. Whatever later affected Robinson,
these basic experiences can be traced throughout his career as a
poet: his deep involvement in the human situation and in the
relation of man to man.

That he would make a career of writing Robinson was
certain some time before he entered Harvard University. In the
Colophon article (165), composed in 1930, he recalled that it
was about the year 1889 when he realized, "and not without a
justifiable uncertainty as to how the thing was to be done," that
he was "doomed, or elected, or sentenced for life, to the writing
of poetry."[24] But Mrs Richards' account of his poetic efforts in
high school and his own words to Harry DeForest Smith in a
letter of 1893 make one wonder if Robinson's memory had not
strayed somewhat. To Smith he wrote:

The people who interest me are my close associates and the
creatures of my own fancy. I have a dozen or so of the latter
who have kept me company for a long time. Now I want to see
them on paper, and if the fates are will[ing] I propose to before
spring. Perhaps no one will see them save myself, but there will
even then be the satisfaction of knowing that I have done something. But, woe is me! where are the shekels? This feeling of
dependence is hell. You cannot imagine it if you try. I do not
mind so much what other people think, but I cannot help wonder-
ing if I am not making an ass of myself. Two or three years at
the most ought to tell something. If I then find that I have [been]
laboring under a delusion *for the past fifteen years* [italics added],
it will not be too late to start out for an occupation and a living.

It will be another case of a disappointed life, blasted hopes, and the usual accompaniments. Whatever I do outside of literature will be done as a task, pure and simple.[25]

It is clear then that Robinson had pretty well set his course some years before 1889, although by that time he could not envisage any other career. Even had he foreseen the lonely stretch of years that lay ahead for him, it is doubtful that he would have altered his intentions. Nothing that he saw or did during the two years after his graduation from Gardiner High School could have persuaded him to give up a career in "literature." He grew increasingly skeptical of the general run of people in business and, indeed, of many of the people in Gardiner who, he felt, cast critical eyes at him as he walked the streets and who would never understand his interest in poetry. He admitted, years later, to having been "unpractical and indifferent . . . to any of the world's reputable pursuits" so that he could not or, at any rate, did not reveal his plans even to his mother and father.

Thus when his chronic ear condition "kicked up" and made trips to Boston to see a specialist imperative, he found it easier than he had expected to persuade his father that a year or two at Harvard might, after all, be a good thing. In great spirits he wrote Smith on September 13, 1891, that his application for admission had been accepted and that he planned to leave Gardiner about September 27. Entering as a special student was not, he realized, the most satisfactory way of going to college, but it was "better than nothing." It would give him what he had come to believe that he seriously needed: mingling with strangers of varying backgrounds and experiences, facing new situations and conditions, acquiring at least a flavor of college life. For almost twenty-two years, he wrote Smith with a touch of self-recrimination, he had scarcely moved from his own back yard; and such insularity was not wholesome. "Solitude (in the broad sense of the word)," he wrote, "tends to magnify one's ideas of individuality; it sharpens his sympathy for failure where fate has been abused and self demoralized; it renders a man suspicious of the whole natural plan, and leads him to wonder whether the invisible powers are a fortuitous issue of unguided cosmos, or the cosmos itself. . . ."[26] He had had enough, for the moment, of living alone—or so he said. Harvard would be a welcome respite, therefore, not only from a deteriorating situation at home but also, for the time being, from a sense of guilt over his own inability to make a living in what his father and Herman would consider a respectable fashion.

III *Harvard Days*

Robinson's letters to Harry DeForest Smith and Arthur Gledhill during his Harvard days form a fair record of his college activities: his course of study, the grades he earned, his early publication in the *Advocate,* his friends and companions along the way—in short, a kind of documentary of his social, intellectual, and artistic development that is both revealing and rewarding. His adviser, a French professor, Cesar de Sumichrast, registered him for English Composition and Rhetoric, Anglo-Saxon (for the discipline it would give him), Shakespeare, Nineteenth Century Prose Writers, and First-Year French. Scarcely a month later Edwin dropped Anglo-Saxon, the rudiments of which he found "hellish." Shakespeare, a course that might have meant a great deal to Robinson, was a severe disappointment. Professor Child had "an unpleasant penchant for odd usages of words—prolepses, adjective-adverbs, etc.—bewildering his students in examinations by listing a row of them to be explained and illustrated."[27] Robinson was unimpressed, and said so. Although he did well in composition, he was highly critical of the way in which it was taught; and he ridiculed the red-ink "decorations" that he found on the papers returned to him. "Eng. Comp." should be taught, he believed, by the best instructors, not by neophytes. But he worked earnestly for Gates in Nineteenth Century Prose Writers and for Marcou and de Sumichrast in French, men whom he respected and who gave him disciplines he could value.

Slow to make new friends and never immodestly intrusive upon the company of others, Robinson lived for some time a lonely college life. He heard the freshmen on the campus one night, he told Gledhill, practicing a college yell which made the night "most damnably hideous." All the same, he wished to be one of them; and he always regretted not being a regular student, progressing through the college years and graduating with his class (as it might have been) of 1895. He attended a party or two given by Professor and Mrs. de Sumichrast in whose home he made a valiant effort at being the social man, but, for the most part, he found these affairs vapid. The forced nature of the conversation, the apparent lack of sincerity—the struggle to move about, to be introduced, to say the right words—appalled him, filled him with a sense of his own insufficiency. He was simply not cut out for "sociability," and he forever shrank from mixing in large groups. Significantly, the pattern of his friendships first established at Gardiner High School carried over into his college years and into his entire life: he was always much more comfortable in the company of a handful of men companions than in any other kind of social relationship, and he was even more at ease with only one.

However, before the winter was well advanced he had, quite opportunely even if casually, made the acquaintance of a few good fellows, among them some who were to become lifelong friends and intimates. George Burnham, Harold Latham, Mowry Saben, Joseph Ford, William D. Whitney: these are the names most often mentioned in his letters. With Burnham, at least, he was to associate and correspond throughout his lifetime and with the others for many years.

For the most part, Robinson enjoyed the bull sessions held in his own room or in the rooms of his friends. A sampling of incidents that he mentioned in his letters, however, reveals that such sessions were casual rather than habitual. When three of his new-found companions dropped into his room "with a dozen of beer" one January afternoon during his first year, he could say: "We had a very pleasant time for the remainder of the day." On another occasion, Harold Latham startled him into a discussion about life. What does it amount to, anyway? Latham asked. What are we on earth for? What's the point? Unable to answer, Robinson shook his head and "blew a stream of Bull Durham smoke into the air. . . ." But the two went on to discuss the matter for an hour and then went out to dinner together. At times, however, Robinson rebelled. Mowry Saben and Crapo started an argument in his room one evening and kept at it until after twelve. He finally drove them out, later concluding that he had been a fool to put up with the argument so long and that courtesy did not demand such a sacrifice of his time.

IV *Cultural Interests*

But the joys of the theater, the opera, and the symphony concerts in Boston, he soon discovered, and he attended one or the other almost invariably on the weekends. Music had always meant much to him. Earlier in Gardiner his tentative experiments on violin and particularly on clarinet, although they did not turn him to music as a career, had given him some appreciation of the values of orchestral instrumentation. And while he was never to acquire a thorough technical knowledge of music, and never pretended to do so, he was sensitively responsive to it. Music and poetry were to him closely allied as artistic expressions—"music being poetry and poetry being music," as he wrote to Arthur Nevin.[28] Late in his life he even collaborated with two friends, Louis Ledoux and Lewis M. Isaacs, in the composition and publication of "Slumber Song," to which he contributed the "melody," while Ledoux wrote the verse and Isaacs the piano arrangement.

But attendance at concerts and operas, begun while Robinson was at Harvard, was continued throughout his lifetime. "These Saturday nights are about the only real outing I get and I enjoy them," he wrote Smith.[29] What he took with him from the concert hall later found its way into poems, notably "Captain Craig," *The Man Who Died Twice,* and *Tristram,* the latter inspired, in fact, by his love of the Wagner opera. He saw Agnes Huntington in *Captain Thérèse;* Julia Marlowe in *As You Like It, Romeo and Juliet, Twelfth Night, Much Ado About Nothing, Cymbeline; Lady Windemere's Fan;* Modjeska in *Macbeth;* Patti in *Traviata;* and Lillian Russell in *Giroflé-Girofla*—these and possibly other productions not mentioned in his letters to Smith and Gledhill.

But whether it was concert, theater, or opera in the company of his new-found friends or, on occasion, with Alanson Tucker Schumann who visited him several times at Cambridge, he would sit afterward in a local tavern to drink a bottle of two of Guinness's Dublin and to enjoy a round of talk. Such excursions, however, did not interfere with Robinson's studies. He read as widely as ever with the difference that his reading was now better ordered and more purposive. In this first year, too, he kept after his poetry; he had been on the campus scarcely a month when he sent his "Villanelle of Change" to the *Advocate,* in which it was soon published, as was his "Ballade of the White Ship" and later "Supremacy." In a hopeful mood he submitted his sonnet "Thomas Hood" to the *Harvard Monthly,* whose editor was Robert Morss Lovett; and he would have despaired over the rejection of the poem had not Lovett called on him personally to inform him that the *Monthly* rarely printed the work of a first-year man. Lovett urged him to submit other poems, but Robinson failed to publish anything in this periodical.

The *Monthly* was, it appears, almost a closed corporation. Its chief contributors numbered, among others, Lovett himself, William Vaughn Moody, Trumbell Stickney, and even George Santayana, who was then an instructor in philosophy. During the Harvard years, Moody was for Robinson scarcely more than a speaking acquaintance, as was Stickney, although only a few years were to pass before Moody and Robinson became intimates, corresponding frequently until Moody's untimely death. Yet Robinson's first year came to an end, and it had not been strikingly successful. He returned to Gardiner, feeling somewhat depressed (he wrote Smith) and believing that he might have been a quite different sort of person had he entered Harvard as a freshman three years earlier. He returned to Gardiner, unhappily enough, to watch his father die—the first of four deaths to occur in his family during an astoundingly short period.

The summer could not have been either a gay or even a relaxing experience for the youngest of the Robinsons. But he was in a better mood when he appeared again in Cambridge, "this year to work," he told Gledhill; and he confided to Smith that he felt better than he had when he left home earlier in the fall. He set a goal of reading about thirty French books and about twelve German, for he was taking courses in both languages. He had registered also for Philosophy, Eighteenth Century English Literature, and Fine Arts III (a "pipe" course in ancient art) under popular Charles Eliot Norton. He felt himself defeated by Logic, for he was uneasy in the realm of abstract thought. German composition he found unusually difficult. His goals, however, were impressive. "In truth I am starting in as a sort of short-haired grind," he wrote Smith, and then added, "but the long hair will come. Have been here a week and have drunk but one beer."[30]

During this second year he read prodigiously and not only for his courses. He wrote no poetry and did not again attempt publication in the Harvard periodicals. Moreover, during this year his reading took him farther afield than he had ever gone before. He and Smith exchanged magazines to which they subscribed: *Harper's Weekly, The Mahogany Tree,* and *The Nation,* all of which he considered far below the standard of the London

Spectator or the *Athenaeum*. "I cannot understand why it is that America cannot publish a decent review," he wrote Smith. But poetry and fiction—novels especially—he read avidly, even to the point of hurting his eyes. According to library records, Robinson withdrew no more than twenty-one books in two years. From the list of books that he mentions having bought at Schoenhof's and other bookstores, however, it is clear that he preferred owning to borrowing. Of the poets, he mentions most often Kipling and Matthew Arnold; however, on one occasion he sat through a lecture on psychology reading Elizabeth Barrett Browning.

Robinson lived up to his intention to work harder during his second year at Harvard, but at its conclusion he wrote to Gledhill that he was only moderately well satisfied. Toward the end he was "grinding" for examinations that he "found no possible use of taking." To Smith he wrote that, although he had profited from his experience, he had no special desire to return another year. He seemed to think that he had "got comparatively little" from his two years, but he had gained more than he could have gained in Gardiner in a century. Almost a year later upon reflection, however, he wrote Smith: "It positively frightens me when I think of the opportunities, small and great, which I lost while in Cambridge; but then, I am thankful for what little I got, and feel that my life is infinitely larger for my going there . . . as you must know what those two years were to me, who had lived like a snail for twenty years before."[31]

What value Harvard had for Robinson, then, lay not so much in the course work that he took, though the orderly discipline he received in some of his classes unquestionably strengthened him. Academic life had not proved to be the winy draught of learning and inspiration that his enthusiasm had led him to think it would be. Its value lay more in supplying those very needs that he confessed to having even before he left Gardiner: the broadening of his associations, the breaking down, for a time at least, of the insular existence of his own mind.

What kind of poetry Edwin Robinson might have written had he been more the hail-fellow social man no one can say. What he *was* then shadowed forth what he was to become: *not* a man hopelessly isolated in an inhuman society—although there were moments when he thought himself to be so—but a man who by nature or by studied preference turned away from people in the group or the mass. Robinson's comment to Smith in the spring of 1893, buried in a letter but oddly pertinent, should be noted: "It was enough to do a man's soul good to sit in the Common or Public Gardens yesterday afternoon. . . . I had an engagement at four, but went in early to have a smoke and watch the people. People are rather interesting after all, if you don't have to talk with them."[32] This statement contains the essence of the man and the pattern of life that he was to develop. If we add to his inherent shyness and his taciturnity the rather devastating circumstances of his life of the next twelve years or so, we see what effect Robinson's development would have upon his poetry: his poems would tend to be ingrowing, analytical.

CHAPTER *2*

The Gold I Miss for Dreaming

LOOKING BACK at his two years in Cambridge, he admitted
to Gledhill, as he had to Smith, that he was glad to have
had the experience. He confessed, however, that if affairs at
home had been happier, he could have enjoyed himself even
more.[1] In Gardiner once more, whether for better or for worse,
he determinedly furnished a room in his mother's house with a
semblance of comfort and settled down to what he hoped would
become a successful career as an author. He had an itch for
writing, he wrote Gledhill, that was "worse than the devil" and
that had spoiled him for any other occupation; for "writing has
been my dream ever since I was old enough to lay a plan for
an air castle."[2] Now he seemed to think that he had a good
opportunity to make a beginning; if he failed in this enterprise—
and he knew that his chances of success were not great—he would
regard his life as a disappointment and a failure. Only indirectly
did he refer to Herman's recent financial reverses in the Mid-
west: "My money has all gone to the devil in a bad investment
and I am poor as need be. But that is all right. The loss of money
is a small thing after all, compared with other things."[3] Gardiner
and its people had no charms for him at this moment in his
life—nor for Herman, ever the materialist, who started drinking
to forget his misfortune.

The letters that Robinson wrote in those early years to Gledhill and Smith most often reveal a mind in search of understanding, of "light," as the poet called it, of certitude, of meaning.
They are confessions of his ambitions, his doubts, his evaluations
of things said and written; they contain critical comment, as
was his habit to write them, upon books and poems that he had
read. But when both these friends married, the correspondence
gradually ended. Although the inner man appeared in the youth-

ful exchange, as Ridgely Torrence remarked, "we soon read no more in that book. With this key he did not unlock his heart."[4]

His personal history appears nowhere at all. The inner Robinson is kept a closely guarded secret. And so, as it were, he lived two lives: one private and known to only one or two members of the family and possibly to an intimate or two; the other no more than partly public for, never given to self-revelation, through the years Robinson grew increasingly laconic. Not Torrence nor Burnham nor Herbert Gorman nor Mason nor Moody—none, probably could have unlocked his heart, good friends that they were. What he may have talked about to intimates like Smith or Ed Moore is also unrecorded, but it is unlikely that he said very much. He was, on the other hand, quite willing to talk or to write letters about the composition of poetry which, he said himself, was all that he knew how to do.

But it is worthwhile briefly to record something of Robinson's early attempts at prose; for he wanted to succeed as a writer and recognized the fact that he could not easily make a living from the writing of poetry. He tried his hand at short stories after the manner of the French *contes* or sketches and sent some of them to the *Atlantic Monthly*. The editors regarded them as having merit, but they nevertheless rejected Robinson's tales. Poetry inevitably intruded. To Harry Smith he proposed a new translation of Sophocles's *Antigone,* Smith setting it down in prose and Robinson creating a new poetic version. The manuscript of that youthful attempt was afterward destroyed, although the work of the translating went on for several years. Meantime, Robinson experimented with French forms of poetry and with sonnets. Outside of his writing, there were additional problems. If he entertained serious hopes about Mabel Moore, the sister of his boyhood companion Ed Moore, he must have been distressed to see their relationship come to a sudden end. The French lessons that he had begun with her early in the year 1894 were over by May; and it must be assumed that, while he may have been in love with her, she rejected his suit. So, at any rate, he implied in a letter to Harry DeForest Smith. Three weeks later Smith announced his engagement to be married, and Robinson was unquestionably devastated. Bravely enough he wrote to his friend that he had known for some time that the marriage was coming; but, with Gledhill already married, he realized that he soon would have no intimates to whom he could look for sympathetic understanding of his unrealized hopes, with whom he could discuss poetry or the latest novels he— and they—had read. At the moment there was no one in Gardiner whose friendship counted; and Butler, Saben, Latham, Burnham, and other of his Harvard friends were scattered.

At twenty-four, he wrote Smith, he was completely dependent upon his mother for every penny he had to spend, for the food he ate, and for a room of his own in the big house on Lincoln Street. In his twenty-fifth year he still had no prospects, almost no money, and very little hope. He admitted that he simply lacked the courage to give up all that he had determined to accomplish; yet, if he capitulated, he could foresee only an odd-job, hand-to-mouth existence for the rest of his life.[5] In the same vein he wrote Smith a few months later: "When the time comes to put away childish things, the individual stands in a new light. . . . The man has come and taken the boy away. . . . This is something the way of it with most people, I fancy, but somehow I, with my crotchets and my childish sensibilities, cannot put away the old things."[6] The comforting and comfortable pattern of his life in Gardiner with the friends of his youth to "chin" with, smoke with, walk with, was destroyed. Robinson knew it; for he wrote in one of his "Octaves":

> We lack the courage to be where we are:—
> We love too much to travel on old roads,
> To triumph on old fields; we love too much
> To consecrate the magic of dead things,
> And yieldingly to linger by long walls
> Of ruin. . . .

He still was afflicted with his "runny" ear; and, for a time after he left Harvard, his eyes gave him so much trouble that he was forced to limit his reading. But despite his afflictions, he held fast to the conviction that he would somehow succeed. In the spring of 1895 he told both Gledhill and Smith that, although he was spiritually depressed, his courage was by no means diminished. Lippincotts had accepted his sonnet on Poe, and not all hope was lost. By August he could write Arthur Gledhill: "I shall never be a Prominent Citizen . . . but I shall be something just as good and perhaps a little more permanent."[7]

I *The Torrent and the Night Before (1896)*

Something "more permanent" did in fact seem possible to Robinson by November when he told Gledhill to expect, some time within twelve months, a volume of his verse. By February, 1896, he readied a small manuscript, named it *The Tavern and the Night Before*, and sent it off to the publishers. Two months later it came back and by the end of summer, it had been rejected twice. The second publisher had seen "John Evereldown," "Luke Havergal," "The Dead Village," and the Verlaine sonnet, among a number of other poems; but these poems were not considered good enough for publication. With the help of an uncle, Edward Fox, Robinson then arranged for a private printing of his manuscript, newly entitled *The Torrent and the Night Before*, an edition of three hundred and twelve blue paperback copies that cost him fifty-two dollars. He promptly mailed them to friends, to people whose interest in poetry might lead them to read his work, and to numerous critics who, he hoped, might find something to their liking.

The poet's own evaluation of his effort is difficult to assess, for it contains the contradictions of uncertainty, the fluctuations of hope and despair. He maintained to Gledhill that in writing the poems he had "let tradition go to the deuce." There was in fact nothing of the usual tinkling quality of popularly printed poetry in them. In one paragraph to Smith he could say, on the one hand, that he wished he could kick the whole stack of printed copies as far as Augusta and "never see them again," yet, on the other hand, maintain that they might "amount to something some day." "I cannot judge my own work at all," he concluded. "I doubt if anyone can who writes anything."[8] He confessed to Smith, shortly after the publication of *The Torrent* that the future looked as dark as ever to him even if he had greater courage than before to look into it.

Some praise came, however, to elate and to bolster him—to give him the prodding he wanted and needed. His letters to Smith from December 22, 1896, through March of the following year comprise a record of comments made by friends and critics.[9] A few responses must have made him believe that he had substance. Barrett Wendell wrote, thanking him for the poems and saying, "Very rarely, I think, does one find such work as yours—

where every line that meets the eye proves itself at a glance real literature."[10] Horace Scudder, another whose name meant something to Robinson, said, "May I express my pleasure at poetry which has so much warm blood in its veins?"[11] But the comment of the author of *The Hoosier Schoolmaster* elated him. "I don't thank you for sending me a book," Edward Eggleston wrote, "for I get books of poetry until I haven't shelf-room for them. But you have given me a rare sensation: you have sent me a book that I can read, and for that I thank you. I am a very busy man, but you have sent me a book I cannot help reading and for that I forgive you. . . . Let a total stranger hail you with admiration, putting aside all flattering words of which you have no need, for which you have no desire. . . ."[12]

Not all the comment was uniformly good. S. Weir Mitchell, who reserved final judgment, thought that the poems showed promise but not fulfillment; and he advised Robinson: "You will do better if you are yet young."[13] The Chicago *Record* exclaimed ". . . Mr. Robinson succeeds in shattering many remarkable and hitherto respected laws of versification."[14] And as might have been expected, many of the best-known magazines ignored his thin little volume. He realized that what he needed most was a reputable publisher, for a privately printed collection could not command the attention of important reviewers and critics; and without that mark to distinguish him, he could not hope for a reading public. By May, 1897, he admitted to Harry Smith that *The Torrent* had stopped flowing. He hoped to get it started again in the fall by adding some water; and if it proved to be anything stronger than water, that would be even better. In any case, he could not afford to rest on a single and fleeting accomplishment.

Perhaps the Richard Badger Company of Boston was not the best of all possible publishers for Robinson's next venture; it was a kind of "vanity press"—the author had to share the cost of printing—but the poet yearned for a wider audience and believed that Badger might prove the proper stimulus. Fortuitously, a Harvard class-mate and good friend, Will Butler, offered to underwrite the printing of five hundred copies of the new collection, along with an additional fifty copies bound in vellum. Robinson deleted from *The Torrent* a number of lesser poems and added several that now are among his best known. "Kliff Klingenhagen," "Richard Cory," "Fleming Helphenstine,"

"The Pity of the Leaves," and the twenty-three Octaves over which he had labored meticulously—among others—now found their way into print. The new volume was published under the title *The Children of the Night*.

II *Family and Friends*

Meanwhile, he had found a few new friends in Gardiner, and for a time they made life tolerable for him there. He had sent a copy of his first collection of poetry to Laura Richards, a daughter of Julia Ward Howe; and soon he was invited to the Richards' home. Laura Richards, an intelligent and outgoing woman, became one of the poet's most faithful friends and correspondents all through his life. In after years her *E. A. R.* (1936), a brief biographical sketch of Robinson, became a warm testimonial to their friendship and revealed her devotion to him and to his poetry. She introduced him not only to her immediate family, in whose company he spent so many happy hours, but also to the Gardiners (after whom the town, Gardiner, had been named). It was in the Richards' home, too, that he met their cousin, John Hays Gardiner, with whom he developed a firm friendship. Hays Gardiner, a Harvard faculty member, very substantially helped the struggling poet in the publication of some of his work; and, in the black and despairing years that Robinson later experienced, he dipped generously into his pocketbook to save his young friend from almost total penury.

The death of his mother just before *The Torrent* was published and the continuing deterioration of his older brothers weighed heavily on Robinson. By comparison, the gaiety, the sheer delight in life that he found in the Richards' home was almost too much for him. He wrote Harry Smith: "The only trouble with that family is they are too abnormally happy and unconscious of the damnation that makes up nine tenths of life."[15] Only a month earlier he had advised Smith in a dark philosophical moment: "Nine tenths of the happiness in the world (if there is any) is due to man's ignorance of his own disposition. The happy people are they who never had time to think it over."[16] Mrs. Richards would have understood, unquestionably, had she read those words. But the thought reinforced in his contemplation soon found its way into the portrait of the debutante

in "Captain Craig"—contradictions and incongruities that were
etched in his remembering mind:

> "Now, you see,
> There goes a woman cursed with happiness:
> Beauty and wealth, health, horses,—everything
> That she could ask, or we could ask, is hers,
> Except an inward eye for the dim fact
> Of what this dark world is. The cleverness
> God gave her—or the devil—cautions her
> That she must keep the china cup of life
> Filled somehow, and she fills it—runs it over—
> Claps her white hands while some one does the sopping
> With fingers made, she thinks, for just that purpose,
> Giggles and eats and reads and goes to church,
> Makes pretty little penitential prayers,
> And has an eighteen-carat crucifix
> Wrapped up in chamois-skin. She gives enough,
> You say; but what is giving like hers worth?
> What is a gift without the soul to guide it?
> And there she goes,
> Like a whirlwind through an orchard in the springtime—
> Throwing herself away as if she thought
> The world and the whole planetary circus
> Were a flourish of apple-blossoms. Look at her!
> And here is this infernal world of ours—
> And hers, if only she might find it out—
> Starving and shrieking, sickening, suppurating,
> Whirling to God knows where . . . But look at her!

The bleak portrait limned faithfully those extreme moments
of doubt that Robinson experienced. Yet all was not dismal and
dark, even in Gardiner. He developed a happy companionship
with Arthur Blair, a banker, Linville Robbins, a young man
interested in geology, and Seth Pope, who had been teaching but
who for the time being had no school. They called themselves
the Quadruped, and they met evenings to enjoy one another's
company in talk and play. Blair's fiddle and the long discussions
made their way into "Captain Craig" and other Robinson poems.
The poet used the Quadruped clubroom often during the day-
time in order to escape from his room in the Lincoln Street
house, where the atmosphere sometimes distressed him.

But even with the new-found friends, Gardiner was not,
could not be, a happy place for him to live and write in. His

brother Dean was slipping gradually away; Herman was now drinking heavily. His wife Emma and her three little girls accounted for whatever sanity remained in that unfortunate home. Win Robinson could be counted out; he was not a practical man. He did his absent-minded share of the jobs about the house, where they were all living. Perhaps he cared too much for his brother's wife. Perhaps she leaned too much upon him for support and comfort in her own desperate hours. Perhaps he longed to be in the center of larger activities where he could find kindred poets and writers for inspiration. In any event, he could not remain longer in Gardiner. New York tempted him. Some friends, like George Burnham, were there. Opportunities to meet publishers, Harvard classmates, and other acquaintances—all were there. And New York it was to be. His departure for the great city marked a significant turn in his life.

III   *New York*

For the next thirty-six years, New York became a beginning and an ending of the limited circuit Robinson rode: New York to Boston to Gardiner to Peterborough and back again to New York—to the last days of his life. Until his first visit to America's largest metropolis, Gardiner had served the poet as a backdrop for all the dramas his men and women were to play in. And it was to remain his chief stage; but it was in New York where he met Alfred Hyman Louis, the failure-hero of his first long poem, "Captain Craig."

Most fortuitously, though inadvertently, Robinson read in *The Century Magazine* a quatrain written by a New York man, Titus M. Coan. He had sent a copy of *The Torrent* to Coan and in return had received an invitation to visit in New York. In Coan's office he found Craven Langstroth Betts who years afterward wrote a memoir of Robinson, now housed, uncompleted and unpublished, in the Williams College Library. He met Alfred Louis and Edith Brower there, too. He stayed with Burnham, his longtime Harvard friend. But of all his early associates in the great city, Alfred Louis claimed his first attention.

Louis was sixty, an English Jew, Cambridge educated, and phonomenal. During his life in England he claimed to have known nearly every great figure of his day: George Meredith,

George Eliot, the Rossettis, Herbert Spencer, Thomas Huxley, John Stuart Mill. In the United States he knew William Dean Howells and Henry Wadsworth Longfellow and an endless number of lesser lights. He was, or had been, lawyer, poet, politician, musician, prophet; and he was now living a hand-to-mouth existence, spared starvation by his friends who fed him and who understood and accepted his criticism when he turned on them. He hated the United States; he both loved and hated England. In the end, a number of generous friends took up a collection so that Louis could cross the Atlantic to die in his native land.

But, despite all that he was or was not, his conversation—often only a monologue—stimulated and excited his listeners: he stirred the imagination, challenged the intellect, inspired the creative. Win Robinson, still suffering from a famine of companionship of minds in Gardiner, was mesmerized by the older man's erudition. Pauper though Louis had become, a failure in most men's eyes, Robinson thought that he was a genius. Others might scoff, but the young poet listened and learned, and made a hero of the old man; and thus was "The Pauper"—later "Captain Craig"—conceived in Win Robinson's eager, expanding mind. But, to use Robinson's own expression, the creature was slow to be born and even slower to grow and walk about in his frayed coat with its grimy collar. The manuscript of "Captain Craig" became, finally, as tattered as its protagonist and was scarcely known to more than ten men before it found its way into print. In the meantime, *Children of the Night* gained some quick recognition, flashed briefly in the eyes of a few discerning critics, and shortly lost all the momentum that Robinson had hoped it would develop. Only *The Nation* and Chicago's *Chap-Book*, among the more influential magazines, gave Robinson's new collection the kind of critical comment that he needed and that his poems deserved. Most of them, like *The Independent*, *The Critic*, and *The Bookman*, ignored him.

He left New York for Gardiner in the summer of 1898. But he still was uncomfortable at home, facing Dean's increasingly weakened condition and Herman's indifference, if not his open antagonism. For a time he stayed with Arthur Blair in nearby Winthrop, working on "Captain Craig." By November, however, he apparently was back again in the Lincoln Street house. He had earlier finished his "Old Maid," later called "Aunt Imogen";

now, he wrote John Hays Gardiner that "Pauper" was nearly all written in rough draft, although he needed about six months of uninterrupted labor to "fix" it. When Hays Gardiner persuaded Harvard's President Eliot to employ the young Maine poet as an assistant in his office, Robinson wrote, on November 2: "I am very glad to learn that there seems to be some shadow of a chance for me in Cambridge, and I feel, naturally, that I ought not to be too independent in regard to the conditions."[17] Although Robinson would have preferred to start his work with President Eliot at a later date, the position was open to him in January, 1899, and he took it without much hesitation.

He soon found, however, that he could not work in the president's office and write more than a few lines of poetry in his spare time, no matter that his duties were merely routine. Robinson made a botch of the job of office boy before he was through with it, six months later. He lacked a capacity to adjust to new situations, and there was no square corner in his imagination that would permit him to develop the little skills he needed. He confessed his failure to Gardiner and apologized for it. Months after he had left Cambridge, he admitted to his benefactor, who was then in Europe, that he liked Cambridge very much indeed, but liked New York better when November came. He fancied that he might like Switzerland, too; but, he said, in a comment redolent with his dry wit and typical of him: "I'm not sure of my capability of adapting myself to the ways of other peoples. It may be for that reason that I have not yet been in Brooklyn—"[18] He was not cut out for much of anything but the writing of poetry—and he said so over and over again. But he could write poetry even if he starved in the process.

While at Cambridge, however, he made some new friends and renewed association with older ones. Daniel Gregory Mason was among them there and was throughout his lifetime one of Robinson's closest friends and admirers. The poet went to Dorchester to meet Josephine Peabody, a young poet with whom he was to correspond for a long time. He liked her, but was not sure whether she liked him or only his poetry. In August he confided to William Vaughn Moody, with whom he now had become a warm associate, "I have seen Miss Peabody six or seven times, but the eternal bumpkin in me is a little more than she can stand and a little more than I can overcome. If you write a treatise on the Subjugation of the Agricultural Exterior, I will buy a dozen copies. I used to think that James [Henry James] was wrong in his remarks on the formation of character—which includes 'neckties and pants' as well as total abstinence—but I am beginning to think that he might have gone farther than he did. . . ."[19] But if Robinson saw his flaws clearly, he had not learned to eradicate them. Habit and reticence and an obstinate tenacious clinging to the known and the familiar were inhibiting elements in his life.

In September, 1899, Dean Robinson died, a scant three years after his mother had been laid in her grave, and Edwin went home for the funeral. That tragic fall—tragic because Dean's great potential as a physician had, the younger brother knew, been wasted by addiction—depressed and devastated him. As a boy, Win Robinson had idolized Dean. Now, a man, he could estimate more perceptively the human equation.

But Robinson submerged his unhappiness in activity. A month later he was back in New York, living with George Burnham, working away at "The Pauper" ("Captain Craig") and other poems in a forgetfulness of the past and with a determined hope for the future. The shock of a complete change of scenery would probably have done him good, but his pockets were nearly empty and were to remain so for a good many years. In April, 1900, he wrote Hays Gardiner, "I am glad you are going to Europe. I am going sometime, but I don't know when. Probably about the time I get a new hat."[20] That may have proved to be an accurate forecast. He finally went to England in 1923, and he may have purchased a new hat for the journey.

IV   *Captain Craig* (1902)

In New York, however, he could talk again to Alfred Louis and learn more from the precocious oldster. By the following May he completed his final draft of "The Pauper," named it "Captain Craig," and sent it off to Scribner's. When Louis read the poem, he wept over it, realizing that he was immortalized in its lines. Scribner's rejected it; and, at the suggestion of Daniel Mason of Cambridge, Robinson sent it hopefully to the Boston firm of Small, Maynard and Company. There it languished. Worse, it was left in a Boston brothel by a lustful but forgetful reader for the Boston publishing house; months later, the amorous adventurer returned to his haunt to find that the madam had cached it against his reappearance in her "rooms."

In May, Robinson told Moody he thought that "Captain Craig" was a "more or less valuable piece of property." By December, he wrote Hays Gardiner that he was going to ask for the return of his manuscript from Small Maynard, complaining against their disregard of the "decencies," but admitting that the delay might simply be credited to his inexperience. Later in the year he thought that he would have to send a "relief expedition" to see what had happened to his poem. When he finally had it in his hands once more, Gardiner offered to see whether Houghton, Mifflin might be persuaded to publish it.

Meanwhile, Robinson had completed his tale of George Annandale ("The Book of Annandale"), a poem that he had almost certainly begun shortly after his mother's death. "Isaac and Archibald" he finished and sent to Scribner's who, again, turned him down. He then decided to combine these two poems with "Captain Craig" and add others—"Sainte Nitouche," "The Octaves," and such fine sonnets as "The Growth of 'Lorraine'" and "The Sage." Gardiner and Laura Richards supplied the money for the publication of the collection; and Houghton, Mifflin undertook the printing on a commission basis. But the new book, named *Captain Craig*, found only a cool reception in the hands of the critics and brought its maker no new market for his poetry. For nearly ten years, between 1896 and 1905, he failed to place even so much as a sonnet in American magazines.

Looking back at the critical comment about *Captain Craig* (and other poems), one can only be amazed at the lack of perception that the commentators revealed. Their slavish devotion to the traditional, ephemeral, tinkling, soporific little verses of so many popular writers of the day and their pretense to omniscience would irritate and dismay the most complacent of modern-day readers. They found Robinson's poetry obscure and his blank verse little more than prose set in rough iambic pentameters. They regarded the title poem as formless and devoid of almost everything associated with poetic diction.

Had Robinson's structure been revolutionary, one might have expected such critical taunts. But his forms were quite traditional, even if the subjects of his poems were not in the traditional vein. One does not find much "tinkling water" or many "red-bellied robins" in anything that he wrote. He had long before stated his artistic credo to Harry DeForest Smith: "I prefer men and women who live, breathe, talk, fight, make love, or go to the devil after the manner of human beings. Art is only valuable to me when it reflects humanity or at least human emotions."[21] Robinson hoped to inject a new vitality into American poetry; and he regarded *Captain Craig* as an entirely fresh approach to the human equation—as indeed it was. In addition to an intensity in the develoment of Craig's character, there was a compression and precision of language—aspects of the poem the critics failed to note. They also failed to note the humor in the poem.

But their failures brought no success to the young poet. He faced the blackest moment in his entire poetic career; he faltered; he drank to forget, to dispel insomnia, to stiffen his courage. In debt and living off the generosity of friends, he was afraid that, like his own prototype for failure, Captain Craig, he might become a parasite. When George Burnham suggested a job on the subway project, the first underground rail line to be tunneled in New York, Robinson could not possibly reject the idea. Burnham's brother, an engineer, employed the poet as a time-keeper at two dollars a day for a ten-hour shift.

In the fall of 1903 he went down into the "hole," as he called it; but the world above was not much brighter to him. Foreign as the labor was to his poetical mind, and hard as the physical exertion became—stumbling through the tunnel with a lantern, on his feet most of the time, breathing the dank and gaseous air that rushed at him—he endured his nine-month stint. Whisky helped, as did the "free" lunches at the bar. In January, 1904, he told Hays Gardiner, who was distressed over Robinson's plight, that he "believed" in the subway—for the time being, anyway. "If I were to come out of my hole now," he wrote, "I should feel that I was making the mortal blunder of my life. Some time in the future, when my new book is ripe, I may possibly let you help me out, if it is necessary. But in the meantime I know I am right in the course that I have taken."[22] The book was not ripe, not even ripening; and he spent his free time in the convivial companionship of George Burnham, Ridgely Torrence, and a few other friends. When the subway was finished in August, he came out, undismayed by his experience in the molehole, to go to work on his poetry.

V *The Customs House*

The medieval writer had no compunction about retelling a good story. Often he improved upon the original, as Chaucer is thought to have bettered Boccaccio's *Il Filostrato* in his version of Troilus. But, while the tale of how an American President rescued a young poet from oblivion bears repetition, it can hardly be improved upon. A young Gardiner man by the name of Henry Richards, Jr., happened to have as one of his students at Groton a son of Theodore Roosevelt. The boy, Kermit, conferring with his instructor about books to read, came away from his conference with a copy of *The Children of the Night*. He was so impressed with the poetry that in January, 1904, he sent one of the copies that he had ordered from its publishers to his dynamic father in the White House. Roosevelt was so impressed that he wanted to meet Robinson; moreover, upon finding that the Maine poet was in serious financial straits, he wanted to help him.

Moody wrote Edwin on March 31, 1905: "It may interest you to know that you have been discovered by the national administration. Roosevelt is said to stop cabinet meetings to ask Hay, 'Do you know Robinson?' and upon receiving a negative reply, to spend the rest of the session reading 'Captain Craig' aloud. R. W. Gilder, who told me this, stands in with Teddie, and has promised at my suggestion to tell him you ought to have a nice lazy (Oh, he won't say 'lazy' to Teddie) berth in the consular service in England."[23] Roosevelt did in fact make two offers to Robinson for positions that would have taken him out of New York, but the poet declined. Finally, he confided to Hays Gardiner:

> You will be interested, I think, to know that T. Roosevelt is on my trail again. This time it would seem that he has brought me down with the probability of an appointment as special agent of the Treasury in "New York, or possibly in Boston." [Robinson had indicated to T. R. his preference for a local post.] I don't know a special agent of the Treasury from the mother of Samson. All I know is that it means two thousand a year, "with plenty of time for my own work." [*sic*] If all this comes to pass I may be able to own two pair of shoes at the same time.[24]

Robinson took over a New York Customs House post in June, 1905; but, never one to be content with half-hearted measures, the President went further. He persuaded Scribner's to buy the publishing rights to *The Children of the Night* and re-issue it. He wrote his own critical appraisal of the book for *The Outlook*, thereby inviting the wrath of the whole fraternity of critics who damned him for his intrusion and told him, in effect, to mind his administrative business and to leave the criticism of literature to those who knew something about it. Unquestionably, Roosevelt's enthusiastic appreciation of Robinson's work strengthened his faltering, modest ego; but even the support and influence of a President of the United States did not widen his audience perceptibly or encourage magazine editors to make a habit of printing his poems. Nor did the Customs House position inspire the Muse. Instead, with the freedom from debt it gave him and the inviting prospect of good food and drink, he became something more of the social man. But he still found it necessary to drink in order to relax and be at ease, even with his close friends. With enough whisky in him, his words flowed smoothly; his conversation was brilliant. In other respects alcohol appeared not to affect him at all.

VI   *Adventure into Drama*

Robinson's duties at the customs office were negligible. He had been appointed, he knew, not to serve as a special agent for the United States Government but to write poetry. But the poetry did not come, or at any rate he very nearly abandoned it during his tenure at the New York post; and he found himself caught up in the burgeoning interest in the drama. He saw other men, probably no more competent than he, making names for themselves as playwrights: Clyde Fitch, Eugene Walter, David Belasco, Augustus Thomas, Langdon Mitchell. His friend Moody and Percy MacKaye were both producing; and Josephine Peabody had successfully staged her *Marlowe* at Radcliffe College in 1905. Moody was at work on the first part of what was to be a trilogy of poetic dramas when he and Robinson were at Cambridge in 1899. The two corresponded at length regarding Moody's *The Masque of Judgment*, and there can be little doubt that Robinson was inspired to turn his creative efforts toward the stage. If he had needed an incentive, the phenomenal success of Moody's *The Great Divide*, which opened in October, 1906, and ran for two years, gave him one.

Yet the truth was that, whatever protests he had made to the contrary and with whatever contempt he had expressed for the money-grubbers, Robinson saw clearly that he could not depend forever upon a government "subsidy" or upon handouts from generous friends. He desperately needed to rest his career on something more substantial than the pauper's income that his poetry had so far provided. With three volumes in print, he had succeeded in achieving a repuation as a "minor" poet; yet it was not the need for money only that drove him to the theater. He was living the greater part of his life now in the very center of theatrical activity.

No wonder, then, that Robinson spent the next four years (1905-1909) on his adventures into drama; and, although for a brief interval he returned to poetry, he was before long at work over two plays, *Van Zorn* and *The Porcupine,* neither of which has been given more than scant attention. *The Porcupine,* at least, scarcely warrants the cavalier dismissal that it was given, despite its flaws; and the situation in *Van Zorn* (which is a comedy of situation rather than of character) is hardly more artificial than is, say, the situation in Langdon Mitchell's *The New York Idea,* which had a successful run in 1906 with Minnie Maddern Fiske as Cynthia Karslake.

Briefly put, *Van Zorn* concerns a handsome young woman, Villa Vannevar, who discovers that she is planning to marry the wrong man, Weldon Farnham, an artist. Her discovery, however, is manipulated by a rather nebulous figure, Van Zorn, who turns her mind and heart back to the man whom she had once loved and whom she realizes at last she still loves.

Certainly this play does not come off well. Its characters move on and off the stage stiffly and sometimes without sufficient motivation. Their lines are often written as if to be read and never spoken; and the prose style is somehow reminiscent of the later Henry James, lacking even a hint of the warmly colloquial language we expect to find in comedy. Van Zorn himself moves unrealistically like a kind of earthbound godhead, arranging people's lives while pretending to have no part in the arrangement. Farnham as an image of the successful artist would be better cast as a banker. George Lucas—a man with a dark past and a life corroded by drink—is too much a plaything of Van Zorn's "Destiny," his reformation incredibly sudden. Villa Vannevar's announced unconventionality, when it appears at all, seems to be more in the clothes she wears than in her actions or her speech; and only at the moment when she realizes that she is making a mistake in her plan to marry Farnham does she move the reader.

But what can be said of the failures in *Van Zorn* does not apply with the same force to *The Porcupine;* for in it Robinson develops a highly complex situation of the sort we find in American plays during the 1920's and 1930's. Rachel, the heroine, had loved and clearly still loves Larry Scammon. But Larry, unaware that she was to bear his child, had drifted out of the community to seek his fortune elsewhere. In order to have a father for her child, Rachel marries Rollo Brewster, a local school-teacher. As the play opens, Larry has returned to his home town a financial success. He wins the affection of Rachel's son, who at the moment is ill, by entertaining the lad with his violin; and, ultimately, he learns that the boy is his own.

A secondary plot involves other characters. Rollo Brewster believes that he is in love with Stuart Hoover's wife, while Hoover, a young attorney, is in love with Larry's sister, Alma Scammon. Blunt Ben Baker, a physician attending Rachel's sick boy, is also in love with Alma. As the plot develops, Larry persuades Mrs. Hoover (actually he bribes her) to run away from Hoover and to seek her happiness on the New York stage—where she longs to be. With her departure, Stuart is free to marry Alma. Before the final curtain falls, Rachel, aware that she has never been a proper wife to Rollo and that, although Larry loves the boy, he does not love her, commits suicide. Thus Rollo is released from what has been at best an unhappy union, and Larry remains to take care of his son. But Robinson's theme in this tragedy is not so much that we are punished for our sins as that destiny shapes man's life. We realize that in this, as in nearly all of his work, Robinson does not judge his characters.

Actually, *The Porcupine* is by no means a bad play. Whatever its faults, it yet has moments of suspenseful action and a not inconsiderable dramatic power. Larry Scammon's recognition of the trouble he has caused and the responsibility that he now faces is a moving and vital scene; and Rachel's decision to take her own life is another. Moody wrote to Robinson on October 12, 1907, saying, "I read 'The Porcupine' over again this morning. As much as it impressed me last night, I was much more profoundly moved today on a second reading, both with its power and its finish. I believe now with you that it will take hold of any old crowd and 'run' to beat all bands, when it once gets a fair start."[25] He also told Robinson that he would get the manuscript into the hands of Charles Frohman, probably the best known theatrical manager at the time and the head of New York's powerful theater trust. Moody wrote not out of friendship only; although he had some reservations about certain aspects of dialogue, he was sincere in his estimate of the whole play.

Frohman, however, rejected *The Porcupine* just as, earlier, Wheeler, manager of His Majesty's Theater in London, had rejected *Van Zorn*. Six years later, in retrospect, Robinson regarded the years he had spent on drama as largely wasted; and he wrote a brief appraisal of his efforts: "It isn't that I can't write a play, so far as technique goes . . . but I cannot hit the popular chord, and for the simple reason that there is no immediately popular impulse in me."[26] But the reason was not so simple as that. For one thing, Robinson had not, as he imagined, developed a sense of movement—tempo. His sometimes over-formal speeches could have been revised by an imaginative producer; and, with a presentation by the better players of the day, even *Van Zorn* might have had a reasonably successful run on Broadway. But neither his comedy nor his tragedy was constructed for a "star" in a period of theatrical history when "star" drama was almost an imperative. Clyde Fitch had learned the lesson well, as had Belasco, Eugene Walter, and Augustus Thomas, all of whom wrote plays designed for particular actors and actresses of the day: George Arliss, John Mason, Robert Hilliard, Blanche Bates, Margaret Anglin, Mrs. Leslie Carter, and the Barrymores, among a great throng of competent and ambitious players, some of whom were on the ascendant, some about to retire from the theater.

For another thing, over a period of nearly twenty years— roughly between 1890 and 1910—the commercial theater had been taken over by a group of enterprising businessmen who soon came to exercise almost complete "control over the entire machinery and art of theater production."[27] The syndicate, or trust, thus strangled the creative as well as the experimental in play writing and forced the stars themselves to capitulate. As Sheldon Cheney remarks: "The dramatist with new ideas or vision found the doors of the theater locked to him. The public saw no more classics, no more experimentally new plays; only what businessmen in New York thought popularly sweet or thrilling enough to survive as 'best sellers.' "[28]

Little wonder, then, that *The Porcupine* was shouldered aside by Charles Frohman—smaller wonder still that Robinson and others like him floundered. Their enthusiasm was no match for syndicate power. Moody's unexpected success with *The Great Divide* depended largely upon the unusual nature of his plot. In no respect could it offend either theater managers or audiences, and it differs little from Belasco's *The Girl of the Golden West* as a kind of popular soporific.

On the other hand, *The Porcupine* could have offended a large segment of the theater-going public. Had Sidney Howard tried to produce his *They Knew What They Wanted* in 1908, it is probable that his play would have been summarily dismissed. For the Realistic drama after the Ibsen manner (and the Norwegian playwright was a favorite with Robinson) had to await a more propitious time for its introduction to American audiences. The subject of illegitimacy that invests both *The Porcupine* and the Howard play could hardly have interested the profit takers who wanted only the "sweet or thrilling" on their stages. Thus, aside from experimental showings before groups of intimates, Robinson's plays were never mounted for commercial tests; and he was never again to try his hand at dramatic production. He wrote Hays Gardiner in 1913: "At last I see the light, and I am going to write another book of poems; and then I shall know to some extent what I am about. I hope I haven't 'got into' you enough to make you feel dissatisfied with my change of plans. . . . I find that I have given the thing a fair trial and that it would be unfair to you as well to myself to waste any more of my life in doing something for which I have come to see I am not fitted."[29]

But unless by his terms "popular chord" or "immediately popular impulse" Robinson had the prevailing trust-controlled theater in mind, his assessment of the failure of his plays was an over-simplification. His letters of this period in his life indicate a general naïveté, and unawareness, not only on his part but also on the part of Moody and other of his friends who were interested in the theater. However, these years of experimentation with the drama form, despite the severe disappointments that they brought him, were not entirely wasted. They developed in him a surer touch in the treatment of dramatic dialogue and in the management of dramatic sequence in his longer narrative poems—a development examined in later chapters.

VII *The MacDowell Colony*

Just how Robinson managed to exist in the few years after he left the customs office is not a matter of clear record. Nor is there any reason here to bring order to the confusion of names of the men and women who helped him and the dates of their contributions. Suffice it to say that Hays Gardiner was one of the most ardent admirers of his poetry and the one who most often supported him financially. Indeed, following Gardiner's early death in 1914, Robinson received a respectable legacy variously reported as from two to four thousand dollars. On several occasions the poet gratefully acknowledged his indebtedness to his fellow townsman. Beginning in January, 1917, the poet received annually a gift of money from a group of anonymous donors; the sums, administered by the New York Trust Company, continued until 1922, when he no longer needed assistance.

Meanwhile, he began in 1911 his regular summer migration to the MacDowell Colony in Peterborough, New Hampshire. Although today artists are usually charged a minimal fee for board and lodging and for the use of one of the sixty studios where they have privacy and isolation for their work, Robinson lived throughout his twenty-four summers in Peterborough without expenses other than his travel and his incidentals. Moreover, while under Mrs. MacDowell's friendly care, he could not often spend what little cash he had on alcohol; for a rule, surreptitiously broken from time to time, prohibited liquor on the Colony premises. But Robinson needed to restrain himself and was glad for an excuse to exercise some self-discipline. "My devil is so far away at present that I can't see him, and the wagon goes without jolting," he wrote George Burnham from Peterborough in August, 1912.[30] Three weeks later he mentioned the ten years of protracted punishment he had given his "insides." And he once told Burnham, in a moment of some levity and perhaps some exaggeration: "The papers say that there are only three gallons of whisky *per capita* in the United States. My share would have lasted about twelve days when I was in training."[31]

By 1913, Robinson was encouraged when the editorial offices of such magazines as *Harper's* and *The Atlantic Monthly* were suddenly opened to him. Probably a younger crop of editors with minds more nearly in harmony with the Maine man's kind of song had arrived. Macmillan published *Van Zorn* in 1914, *The Porcupine* in 1915; and a new revised edition of *Captain Craig* also appeared on the market. In 1916 he published *The Man Against the Sky* and a year later the first of his longer narratives of the Arthurian cycle, *Merlin*. In 1921 he collected the first of three Pulitzer awards granted him; and in 1922 at Yale University he garnered the first of two honorary doctorates that he was to receive in his lifetime. The darkest years were behind him.

His movements from New York to Boston to Gardiner to Peterborough and back again to New York had become an established habit. Only once did he break it. In late April, 1923, he sailed to England. He had thought at one time that he might be there a year or longer, but he remained only three months. And he wrote Mrs. Thomas Sargeant Perry on July 13 of that year: ". . . my real reason for sailing on the 26th is that I have got pretty much what I came for and that my inner voice tells me to get back to Peterborough."[32]

Tristram, in 1927, marks the high point in Robinson's career. It is true that it came out at a moment most conducive to its success as a publishing venture. The Literary Guild, which had just come into being, bought twelve thousand copies from Macmillan for distribution to its members. The name of Carl Van Doren was behind the poem, and it was given widespread circulation. But it is equally true that the poem deserved on its own merits its tremendous popular reading and approval. Robinson was of course astounded and elated over its success. He wrote the English Melville scholar, John Freeman:

> My books [*The Children of the Night,* etc.] did what they could to ruin my London publishers, who, after experimenting with three of them, gave me up, not unnaturally, as a bad investment. Sooner or later, perhaps, someone else equally brave and adventuresome, will take a chance with 'Tristram' . . . It is encouraging, at any rate, to know that a poem that runs to more than 4,000 lines of blank verse can still be read, or at any rate bought, by 27,000 people in three months. I did not expect to see any such thing during my life but had fond hopes of something of the

sort when there should be nothing left of me in my grave but a few bones and buttons. Time may have changed his mind in regard to me, giving me this little illusion of importance as a preparation for oblivion. Such things have happened, and fortunately I am too old to take myself too seriously. If this thing had come when I was twenty-five or thirty, no doubt it would have given me a jingle. But on the whole I haven't much to growl over.[33]

He told Freeman later in the year that his publishers had not recovered from the shock of seeing thirteen printings of the long poem disposed of in six months. He had himself been doubtful about its reception; but he had thought, with characteristic self-deprecation, that *Tristram* was not "altogether a failure."

All his life Robinson was solicitous of others—their needs, their hopes, their griefs, their joys—and warmly tender in his thoughts of them and generous in his acts. *Tristram* brought the kind of financial independence that made it possible for him to do what he had longed to do for others over the bleakest years. But he disliked effusiveness and was suspicious of it, and for that reason he found the outright overt gesture difficult to make; he always chose the quietest way possible to effect his ends. Thus when in 1930 Mrs. MacDowell planned a trip to the Mediterranean on a "freight steamer," he was disturbed that such a frail lady should travel without the comfort and convenience of a regular passenger ship; and he wrote to a friend suggesting that somehow more congenial arrangements—in which he wanted himself to assist—might be made.

Where poetry was involved, however, Robinson insisted upon being completely forthright. He was firm, even with his closest friends, though he invariably couched his criticism in the kindest terms that he could find. Moody came in for his share at an early date in their friendship. Concerning one of his poems, Robinson wrote: "I think the last three verses of the first stanza, however fresh and striking they may seem at first glance, are just a little too 'creative'—not to say feminine (I don't mean effeminate) and illogical. You may not agree with me here; and if you do not, it will be no great matter. But I [expect] you to agree with [me] in showing all sorts of damnation on your occasional, inconsistent and obnoxious use of archaic monstrosities like 'lifteth,' 'doth,' etc."[34] Mrs. Perry herself, one of his dearest older friends with whom he corresponded for years, was the recipient of his prodding. "I am sending back your latest version . . .," he told her, "with a few suggestions that you may or may not approve. But you should, at any rate, revise the two superfluous syllables in the line beginning 'And long to escape, etc.' I could almost wish that you had written the poem without alexandrines, which are as rule rather cumbersome except at the end of a Spenserian stanza, but since you have them you ought, in a poem like this, to have them without variations."[35]

Robinson had standards from which he would not deviate. He did not necessarily expect others to agree with him on matters of form or structure, or always on language. But he did expect them to set standards for themselves and to abide by them strictly. Although he himself used traditional forms, it is a mistake to think that he was opposed to all experiment. Actually, the human element was of greatest significance to him. He told Amy Lowell, the driving force of the Imagists (after she had replaced Ezra Pound as a leader in the movement) that the very best of her "free verse" was exclusively "human" and thus old-fashioned. "I don't care a pinfeather what form a poem is written in so long as it makes me sit up," he said to Miss Lowell in 1916. " 'Imagist' work, *per se*, . . . seems to me rather too self-conscious and exclusive to stand the test of time. I feel pretty confident that if you had to sacrifice one or the other you would retain that part of your poetry that has in it the good and bad solid old-fashioned human qualities that make us all one crazy family of children, throwing things at each other across the table, and making faces at each other in secular seculorum."[36]

In later years his attitude toward the younger poets hardened somewhat. To one young acquaintance who had sent him a sheaf of lyrics to read and criticize, he wrote that the sonnets were worth much more time and care than the poet had given them, and he recommended that they not be hurried into print. "I like your lines 'To the People,'" he said, ". . . but I feel sorry when you have not given sufficient attention to technique—without which the best poetic material goes to waste."[37] In short, Robinson was impatient with mediocrity, with an evident lack of discipline, with carelessness in the writing of poetry. Words did not just drift into the poet's mind; they had to be sought and selected with discrimination. Lines might warble reasonably well, but they would not sing a true song unless they were fined and polished. To Robinson, poetry was best in regular rhythms. Even though he regarded Amy Lowell's free verse as often beautiful, he once told her that it would be far more beautiful if it were metrical.

And on he worked, after his own fashion, turning out one long narrative poem after another in well-trimmed blank verse lines: *Cavender's House, The Glory of the Nightingales, Matthias at the Door, Talifer, Amaranth* and, finally, *King Jasper.* Seemingly, he disappeared into his studio at the MacDowell Colony during the summer and reappeared in Boston and New York in the fall with the manuscript of a new poem in his hands. But at last the "machine," as he often called the body, ran down. He died from cancer on April 6, 1935, in New York Hospital. Though for most of his life his name had been buried in some obscurity, the publication of *Tristram* had made it known. At his death the scores of thousands who had opened his books paid him homage.

CHAPTER 3

Wine and Wormwood:
the Robinson Myth

O NE ASPECT of Robinson's life (what will be termed here the "Robinson myth") needs to be discussed at some length, for it directly concerns a rather large body of his poetry. Until recently, no book or article about Robinson has more than hinted vaguely, though mysteriously, of this facet of the poet's personal history. Some writers have made shrewd guesses; others, if they had any specific information, have had so few facts that they have simply avoided the subject altogether. Early in 1965, however, Chard Powers Smith published a book entitled *Where the Light Falls,* the central intent of which is biographical. The book is, in fact, a memoir; but Mr. Smith has devoted one long chapter to an interpretation of Robinson's basic philosophical attitudes. However, nearly two-thirds of the volume is given over to the revelation of new material concerning Robinson's private life, almost all of it hitherto unpublished. This material the author has presented primarily to fill in the incomplete portrait of the Maine poet, and he has attempted to treat his data in a fair and objective manner. His version of the personal history he calls the "Robinson Legend," a legend about which, over a period of several years, he had gathered information from numerous sources, including members of the Robinson family.

Recognizing some basic disagreements about the authenticity of the story, Mr. Smith uses the terms "The Orthodox Account" to represent what some people believe to be the truth about Robinson as the poet revealed himself in his poetry, and "The Dissenting Account" to represent what others regard somewhat skeptically. But, while the author of *Where the Light Falls* states that he leans toward the dissenters in his own thinking, he treats the orthodox account extensively. All this information is of course helpful to the biographer, and Mr. Smith has made ample use of it to fulfill his central intent to write biography.

Still, another significant aspect of Robinson's personal history also exists: the relationship between that history and the recurring themes that are to be found in Robinson's poems. First of all, some facts of Robinsoniana should be examined. It is true that in the published or available letters that Robinson wrote to Gledhill and Harry DeForest Smith one finds the poet revealed rather clearly; it seems likewise true that when that correspondence ceased, the poet "locked his heart." But Robinson may have written several thousand letters; and not all of them, by any means, have been collected and edited. Nor have all the personal documents been made available for scholarly inquiry. Harvard's Houghton collection, for example, is still not open to unrestrained scrutiny and use. A long-promised edition of the Edith Brower letters at Colby College is yet to be published; and, understandably, permission to cite them is now withheld. It would be useful otherwise to record some of the comments that Robinson addressed to Miss Brower, a Wilkes-Barre, Pennsylvania, woman for whom the poet had both affection and respect. Although other minor collections still need to be sifted, piece by hard-found piece the Robinson puzzle is being put together.[1] Mr. Smith's contribution to the portraiture is significant because he knew the poet well. Ultimately, the whole figure of the man will stand revealed.

We may ask, of course, why so much importance is attached to the letters, to documents, indeed to the known and still-sought facts about the life of the poet. What has *that* to do with his poetry? Ellsworth Barnard, perhaps the best and most thorough of Robinson's critics, has answered the question aptly. "Yet (as all good critics, new and old, acklowledge in practice)," he wrote in his excellent study of Robinson's poetry, "poems are made by persons, and persons are members of a society. A poet does not exist in a vacuum, and his poetry is not made out of nothing. The more we know about his life and character apart from his work, and the more we know about the society to which he has belonged, the more fully and accurately we shall understand what he is trying to do, the more clearly we shall see what his work is like."[2]

In other words, it is not enough simply to ask what the poet is saying in a poem as though the poem existed as an entity, as a thing separate from the poet. Cleanth Brooks made such a suggestion not many years ago. "Modern critics," he said, "tend to force attention back to the text of the work itself: that is, to look upon the poem as a poem, not as an appendage to the poet's biography, nor as a reflection of his reading, nor as an illustration of the history of ideas."[3] To this comment, Leon Edel, as if to reinforce Mr. Barnard's contention, replied: "To force our attention back to the text is a good thing; the close reading of that text is the beginning of all literary study; but it is not the end of it. The text cannot be an 'appendage' to the biography of the poet, for it is an integral part of it; and it is a reflection not only of the poet's reading but his way of experiencing life. And certainly sometimes it may well illustrate the history of ideas as well."[4]

We may therefore reasonably suppose that through an understanding of the life and character of a poet, a knowledge of what shaped him, of what forces directed his work, we can find his meanings and the symbols and the patterns of his poems more clearly perceptible. Certainly such a knowledge not only reduces the frustration that occasionally besets Robinson's readers but also gives the lie to a number of views that have been expressed about him. Reticent he was, manifestly, and always the shy New Englander in a large gathering; but the charge that he was cold, aloof, humorless, is only a half truth. Because he never married, it is assumed that he neither knew nor understood women; and, therefore, it must follow that he could not write about them with discernment. Because of the sometimes puzzling involutions in his poetry, it has been said that he was essentially an "intellectual" poet and that in many of his longer poems he became merely ponderous, talking to himself or to a company of faceless ghosts.

I *A Company of Ghosts*

Robinson lived with and knew a company of ghosts; he began to accumulate them at the time of his father's death, shortly after he had returned to Gardiner from his first year at Harvard. But in all the available published correspondence, he scarcely mentions the members of his family; we find the facts only in the private and unpublished papers of the Robinson family. When these are examined, Edwin Arlington Robinson becomes less an enigma and more a man and a poet in proper focus. Even with the behind-the-scenes glimpses into family history, however, conjecture must still supplant what members of the Robinson family know or believe and are pardonably reluctant to disclose. But what can be learned is traumatic.

The story that has become a myth—varying in details, but according in essentials—involves all the members of Edwin Robinson's family, and some others besides. It embodies Robinson's rejection of both his father and his next older brother, Herman, as well as the materialism that they represented; his love for one woman especially—the always sought but never completely obtainable wife, mistress, beloved; his portraits of Herman, Dean, perhaps Alfred Louis; and the cosmic irony of human failure or the human failure redeemed or saved. The impact of the myth upon Robinson's poetic achievement is direct, incisive. Indeed, its very conditions become significant factors in the poet's development, for he seems to have been so obsessed by them that we find them shafted through the entire body of his poetry.

Briefly, the pertinent details are that, during his high school years, Win Robinson met the beautiful Emma Shepherd, a Farmingdale girl, at a dancing school, and he inevitably fell in love with her. To what extent she returned his love is not certain; there is no record, apparently, of his having dated or courted her during this period, although she sent him flowers on the day of his graduation from Gardiner High School—indisputably an overt sign of affection. At the moment the relationship could hardly have approached marriage, for Win was young, without prospects of a job of any durable kind, his future indefinite. We must assume therefore that whatever he may then have dreamed, he put aside to take a post-graduate course at the high school—as has been noted earlier—during the year 1888-89.

Then in the summer of 1889, Win's handsome, dashing brother Herman returned from St. Louis, where he had gone to secure properties for the Gardiner Savings and Investment Company (in which his father was a partner). He, too, became enamored of Emma and sought her hand. Emma twice broke her engagement to Herman, but she at last married him in February, 1890; and, not long afterward, they left Gardiner to live in St. Louis. It may have been that even Dean Robinson loved Emma, for the suggestion has been made that he tried to commit suicide on the eve of the marriage. In any event, Win himself refused to attend the wedding, saying afterward that he could not bring himself to witness it.

At length, when Herman's speculations in Missouri proved profitless, he went to Minnesota to invest in zinc and copper mines. The famous Jasper mine was one of the latter, a name suggestive of the title of Robinson's last long poem, *King Jasper*, published posthumously. At that moment in American history, the economy was hastening toward a financial disaster that broke, in 1893, into a major depression. The St. Louis investments, along with the Minnesota investments, were wiped out, and the considerable fortune accumulated by Edward Robinson was critically reduced. Herman and Emma returned to Gardiner to move into the family home on Lincoln Street. Indeed, Mary Robinson, Win's remarkable, industrious, though rather frail mother, took care of the entire family, including Win, Dean, and Herman and Emma and their now growing family.

It should be recalled that Edward Robinson had died in 1892, his death occurring after a gradual deterioration, as Robinson's letters to Harry DeForest Smith reveal. In 1896, Mary Robinson died of "black diphtheria"; and, because no mortician would serve, the three sons had to lay her out, dig her grave, and bury her. By 1898, Herman, now holding himself accountable for the despoliation of the family inheritance, was drinking excessively; and within a short time, he was well on his way to becoming an alcoholic. He returned one weekend in that year from a fishing trip in a drunken condition, and Emma helped him up the stairs and to bed. When she came down again, Win held her and comforted her. Later, when Herman got out of bed and came downstairs, he found his younger brother and his wife sitting together on the porch, talking quietly. He accused Win of trying to steal Emma's affections, and the two men went upstairs to carry on a long and bitter quarrel—a rupture that was not, apparently, to be resolved between them. Probably this quarrel is to be seen fictionalized in the fight between Penn-Raven and Roman Bartholow in *Roman Bartholow*. For during the argument, Herman is said to have knocked Win down, though possibly Win may have finally had the upper hand. Soon afterward, however, he left the house to return to New York. Within a year, another family tragedy occurred: Dean Robinson died. It is believed that he administered to himself a lethal dose of the narcotic to which he had so long been addicted.

By 1900, Herman and Emma had separated, evidently at her family's insistence. For some years Herman lived an extremely irregular and unhappy existence, his promising career and his undoubted capacity wasted; and he drifted somewhat aimlessly in and about Gardiner and in other spots in Maine or in Boston or New York. For a time he stayed at the Shepherd cottage on Capitol Island on the coast and afterward he lived in the boathouse attached to the cottage. But infrequently he saw Emma or wrote to her. On one occasion when he and Emma met, he spoke accusingly to her. "You don't love me," he said, "the way I love you. If you were to die, I should never marry again. But if I were to die, you would marry Win." Emma protested, and she promised that she would never marry Win, no matter what the circumstances. Not many years after, on February 4, 1909, Herman did, indeed, die in the Boston City Hospital.

It is somewhat ironic that when Herman needed his brother's help most—or what is more important, when Emma needed it (1905-1909)—Edwin Arlington held the Customs House position in New York. After Herman's funeral, however, Edwin, who had returned to Gardiner from his room in New York, sought Emma; and the two of them went for a long walk. The following September he went to Gardiner to claim her, but manifestly she kept her promise to Herman and rejected the thought of another marriage.

This tragic tale is not by any means the whole account that is to be read and pieced together. Had it been a story and no more, a reader might shake his head sadly and dismiss it. What compels attention is the fact that the events and the more intimate relationships disclosed in the unpublished document closely parallel events and relationships in poem after poem that Robinson wrote, whether in short lyrics and sonnets or in long narrative poems.[5] Such works as *Captain Craig, Roman Bartholow, March of the Cameron Men, Mortmain,* "Late Summer," "Cortege," "Bewick Finzer," "Bokardo," "Flammonde," "Exit," the three Annandale poems, and many others must be considered in connection with the myth. Even the Arthurian romances are directly involved, at least in some portions.

Naturally enough, one should raise the question: how close to reality is this myth? Chard Powers Smith devotes the greater part of his memoir to an effort to identify and relate the myth or legend to the known facts about Robinson and, indeed, about the entire family. What Mr. Smith attempts to prove is the fact that the best answer to the question is to be found in the poetry itself; but both external and internal evidence must be examined.

Much speculation has been made, for example, about the woman—or possibly even the women—in Robinson's life. At the MacDowell Colony, where for twenty-four years the poet spent his summers writing, Robinson became almost a legend. It was generally whispered there that he had had one great love and had lost her. Louis Coxe conjectured that possibly this woman was Rosalind Richards, the daughter of Laura and, as noted earlier, one of Robinson's lifelong friends.[6] The suggestion is plausible enough, for in his early Gardiner years he was a frequent guest in the Richards' household.

However, when Robinson returned to Gardiner after his second year at Harvard, he began tutoring in French Mabel Moore, a sister of one of his best friends, Ed Moore. But before long, and for unexplained reasons, his teaching abruptly halted. He wrote to Harry DeForest Smith on May 1, 1894: "Perhaps you will understand my feeling a [little] better, and perhaps not, when I tell you that my French lessons are over. You may interpret this as you like, but I fancy you will not get far out of the way in your conclusions."[7] Implicit in these lines is the suggestion that Edwin had expressed his love and had been rejected. However, one member of the family insists that there was nothing serious in the poet's relationship with Mabel Moore and that she has in her possession a letter to this effect in Mabel's own handwriting.[8]

II *The Woman in "Cortege"*

So far as his Gardiner years are concerned, these young women were possible candidates for the poet's love. But the myth points to Emma Shepherd as the one likely to have affected Robinson most deeply, and the evidence in his poetry supports that contention. There is, for instance, a little-known Robinson poem called "Cortege":

Four o'clock this afternoon,
Fifteen hundred miles away:
So it goes, the crazy tune,
So it pounds and hums all day.

Four o'clock this afternoon,
Earth will hide them far away:
Best they go to go so soon,
Best for them the grave today.

Had she gone but half so soon,
Half the world had passed away.
Four o'clock this afternoon,
Best for them they go today.

Four o'clock this afternoon
Love will hide them deep, they say;
Love that made the grave so soon,
Fifteen hundred miles away.

Four o'clock this afternoon—
Ah, but they go slow today:
Slow to suit my crazy tune,
Past the need of all we say.

Best it came to come so soon,
Best for them they go today:
Four o'clock this afternoon,
Fifteen hundred miles away.

This poem is seemingly ingenuous and simple, almost, one might add, without substance and with scarcely any meaning. The poet had in mind a particular time (four o'clock in the afternoon) and apparently a specific place (fifteen hundred miles away). Two young people married, or at least very much in love, have died—from what cause the poet does not say. But the lines "earth will hide them" and "Best for them the grave today" suggest that a funeral is about to take place or is actually taking place. The poet believes, for some undisclosed reason, that it is best for them to have died and that they now go to their grave—a grave that "love" made for them so early in their lives. And the time and place and death—the remembrance of the couple—hum persistently through the poet's mind. This reading might suffice, at any rate, for a simple interpretation of what the poem says.

A second reading of the lines strongly suggests, however, that the death involved may be only a figurative one. That suggestion and the lines "Had *she* gone but half so soon" (italics added) give the reader pause. It is possible that the woman in this poem had a special significance for the poet. If so, could not the poem have had a personal meaning or have described a particular relationship? Probably "Cortege," the reader begins to think, involves the poet and the young couple directly. Until recently, almost nothing in any of the biographical or critical material so far published about Robinson concerns this seldom-read poem and nothing has been said about a personal involvement for the poet. But not long ago one member of the family definitely suggested such an involvement. "It must be granted," he wrote, "that Robinson could scarcely have hoped that a poem like 'Cortege' would be fully understood by anyone except a few members of his family. . . . I must apologize for saying no more of 'Cortege' at this time except that it was conceived one black afternoon in the late winter of 1890, when Robinson's brother and sister-in-law left Gardiner after their recent marriage . . . on the four o'clock train for St. Louis—fifteen hundred miles away."[9]

It is more than likely that the poem was not only conceived in 1890 but was also written almost at the moment when Herman and Emma departed for the Middle West. The vague hint of the French form in the poetic structure dates the poem; for, in 1890 and probably for a year or two before then, Win had been meeting, it will be recalled, with Schumann's poetry "Club." At that moment, Miss Swan had led them into French poetry and in the writing of French forms—a fact reflected in such of Robinson's early poems as "Ballade of Broken Flutes" (that he dedicated to Schumann), "Ballade by the Fire," Villanelle of Change," and "The House on the Hill." Robinson long retained his interest in these forms. Even as late as February, 1894, he wrote Harry Smith about "The House on the Hill": "These old French forms always had a fascination for me which I never expect to outgrow."[10]

However that may be, "Cortege" should be read as a personal lyric, its intense emotional overtones suggesting sorrow or, at the worst, despair. The line "had she gone" seems to give a special emphasis to the meaning. For the poet does not mention a "he" or a "him." Thus we can only conclude that the poet is moaning over the departure of the woman he loved, and in this respect the myth confirms such a conclusion. The poem represents, then, the figurative death of the young couple and reveals the depth of the poet's despondency. Otherwise "Cortege" leaves the reader puzzled, although he may have found delight in the musicality of the poem and the suggested rhythm of the train-car trucks as they roll and click along on the rails—much as Emma Robinson once remarked. But with the biographical information supplied, the poem is infinitely more intelligible and more meaningful. Emma Shepherd was irretrievably lost to Robinson—or so it seemed to him at the time; and time reinforced the seeming.

III *The Myth in Other Short Poems*

Were "Cortege" the only poem in which one discovers in Robinson's shadowy involutions the relationships between myth and reality, there would be no need to plumb the mystery further. And were not the poet's complex relationship with Emma Shepherd Robinson reflected in the thematic structure of his poetry, the matter would remain only in the realm of the biographer, not in the purview of the critic. But, as has been indicated, close examination of the poems lends substance to the force of the myth.

"The March of the Cameron Men" is not a substantial poem in the Robinson canon, probably because, like "Cortege," its meaning is hidden in personal allusion. The situation is clear enough: a woman recently widowed requests an old friend, a doctor to whom she once, apparently, had given her affection, to come back to attend her dying husband, although the husband is not to be saved. After the death occurs, the woman and the doctor row far out in a lake adjacent her home. The "doctor" believes that she is ready to marry him, but he is struck finally by the "freezing realization" that she is rejecting his suit and burying his hopes. She sends him away with her blessing and her promised prayers.

The poem fails because the reader finds the motivations for its slight action inadequate; its characters remains strangely anonymous. Robinson chose for his lines an old Scottish song in which to disguise both situation and character; it may be that Emma Shepherd played and sang the lyric to him, in which event she, better than any other reader of the poem, could identify with it and understand its essential melancholy, its low-keyed plaintiveness broken only by the "unearthly ululation of a loon" that "Tore the slow twilight like a mortal yell / Of madness, till again there was silence."

However, the "long walk" taken by Win and Emma following Herman's funeral is paralleled closely in the poem, as are other aspects of their relationship. The poem begins with the setting:

> An autumn twilight on a quiet lake;
> A silent house, with more than silence in it;
> A boat, and a man resting on his oars;
> A woman with him, looking at the shore. . . . .

And the woman says "Row me into the middle of the lake, / Where there shall be no eyes, or possible ears, / To watch or listen." When they are at last far from prying eyes and listening ears, the man says

> "If I was careless once, it was because
> Life made you as you are. How, I don't know.
> No more have I a knowledge to define
> A few not all celestial elements
> That I would not see elsewhere than in you.
> Although a doctor, I would not remove
> Their presence, or transmute them.
>
> "You drove me away once, but I came back.
> I came because you said you needed me—
> Because you called me.
>
>   I had come home again,
> Where no home was for me. I could not stay,
> And could not go; for there was a man dying,
> Unless my skill should save him. It was you
> Who called me back again; and we were there,
> Together where darkness was."

As in "How Annandale Went Out" and "Annandale Again," two other poems relevant to the myth, Robinson used the "doctor" as a disguised figure playing a significant part in his poem. The veiled hint of Robinson in a healer's role can be ascribed only to fancy.

Then comes a challenge so direct that it must have been expressed in something like the very words of the poem. It seems to be Robinson's attitude toward Herman and Emma's marriage and Herman's death:

> "He is not there.
> There's only an old garment all worn out—
> A body that he was glad to leave behind.
> What is he now but one far more a theme
> For our congratulation than our sorrow?
> There was no happiness in him alive,
> And none for you in your enduring him
> With lies and kindness. It was a wrong knot
> You made, you two. . . ."

And the man pleads with the woman:

> "There's more of me,
> Be sure, than a man asking for a woman
> Who would not have him if she doubted him.
> I'm farther from the pliocene than that;
> And you would soon see in my care for you
> How much of care there is in a man's love
> When it is love—which is a little more
> Than any myopic science isolates
> With so much carnal pride."

But the woman replies:

> "I thought, before I thought,
> Before I knew, that I could see fair weather
> For you and me, and only friendliness
> In every natural sign that led me on—
> Till I found nature waiting like a fox
> For an unguarded pheasant. But I saw it
> In time to fly away and save myself,
> And, for my flying wisely, to save you.
> There are some *promises of mine*, I know, [italics added]
> And they are best forgotten. If remembered,
> They would be treasured more if broken and lost,
> Like placeless remnants that are in most houses,
> And in most lives."

This poem contains more than fiction. The meeting after the death of the husband, the "doctor's" plea for the woman's love, the woman's reminding him of promises—all seem to speak of reality. But the lines that follow, spoken out of a distress alive with a kind of anger and impatience, strike the sharp tones of

life as if Robinson had stored up in his memory all the words
that passed between him and Emma after Herman's funeral:

> "Nothing in life appears
> To me of more importance than my knowing
> Just when it was you called me, and for what.
> I saw you, on my journey, in my arms
> At a long journey's end, and saw you smiling;
> And so you were—and you were in my arms.
> Why was all that?
>
> "Was it a shadow playing
> For me when I came back there in the starlight?
>
> "We gambled there,
> And are we both to lose? By God, my lady,
> If I have heard you and have learned your language,
> A quieter place for you than in his house
> Would be a place with him where he has gone.
>
> "You will not like that house when he's not there,
> More than when he was in it."

But when the woman has rejected his plea, all he can say is "'God
—is it you? / And has it come to this? Is this the end?'"

"The March of the Cameron Men" more than any other of
Robinson's products, perhaps, closely parallels the Edwin-Emma
relationship as it is revealed in the myth. Yet echoes of the
narrative appear in other poems, such as "Late Summer." Beneath
the title of the poem, in parentheses, is the term "Alcaics"; and
we wonder whether Robinson was referring to a stanza pattern
and meter employed by Alcaeus or whether he had in mind the
exile from Lesbos, his native isle, that was imposed upon the
poet by the tyrant Pittacus, sometime late in the seventh century
or early in the sixth century B.C. Such lines as the following
seem clearly to relate the poem to Win Robinson and Emma
Shepherd, with Robinson exiled from Emma's affections:

> Why, then, should horrors
> Be as they were, without end, her playthings?
>
> And why were dead years hungrily telling her
> Lies of the dead, who told them again to her?
>   If now she knew, there might be kindness
> Clamoring yet where a faith lay stifled.

God, what a shining handful of happiness,
Made out of days and out of eternities,
    Were now the pulsing end of patience—
Could he but have what a ghost had stolen!

What was a man before him, or ten of them,
While he was here alive who could answer them,
But now the man was dead, and would come again
Never, though she might honor ineffably
    The flimsy wraith of him she conjured
Out of a dream with his wand of absence.

The plea, once again, is that of a man who yearns for a woman whose husband is dead; but even as he addressed his plea to her

    . . . he saw that while she was hearing him
Her eyes had more and more of the past in them;
    And while he told what cautious honor
Told him was all he had best be sure of,

He wondered once or twice, inadvertently,
Where shifting winds were driving his argosies. . . .

But the woman, at last, rejects his plea, saying

"What you believe is right for the two of us
Makes it as right that you are not one of us.
    If this be needful truth you tell me,
Spare me, and let me have lies hereafter."

She gazed away where shadows were covering
The whole cold ocean's healing indifference.
    No ship was coming. When the darkness
Fell, she was there, and alone, still gazing.

In the happily ended "Book of Annandale," published seven years before Herman's death and strangely out of keeping in the Robinson canon, Emma's promise to Herman seems almost to have been anticipated:

                And, ah! yes,
There were those words, those dying words again,
And hers that answered when she promised him.
Promised him? . . . yes. And had she known the truth
Of what she felt that he should ask her that,
And had she known the love that was to be,
God knew that she could not have told him then.

> She had told
> Him then that she would love no other man,
> That there was not another man on earth
> Whom she could ever love. . .
> And he had smiled.

In this poem, Annandale, possibly Robinson himself, has just lost his wife, Miriam (perhaps, symbolically, his mother). But during their marriage, some quirk or fancy has brought him secretly to compose "a curious kind of book" addressed to a woman whose face has again and again appeared to him. For Damaris, the loss has come in the death of her husband, Argan; but, though "it was Argan's ghost that held the string / And her sick fancy that held Argan's ghost," Damaris, through her reading of Annandale's book, is able to untie the knot that binds her to Argan and to find herself free to love Annandale:

> Today she could throw off
> The burden that had held her down so long,
> And she could stand upright, and she could see
> The way to take, with eyes that had in them
> No gleam but of the spirit.

"Mortmain" could be (and certainly suggests) a dialogue between Edwin and Emma in later years. A slight story, lightly touched with irony, it can be revealed by the citing of a few lines; but in this case it is not a husband, nor the memory of a husband, nor promises made that cause the woman to reject the man's suit: it is a "brother."

> Avenel Gray at fifty had gray hair,

> Seneca Sprague
> At fifty had hair grayer, such as it was,
> Than Avenel's—

Seneca protests without insistent vehemence:

> "For more than twenty years
> My search has been for an identity
> Worth Time's acknowledgement;

> What is it in me that you like so much,
> And love so little?

"My perishable angel,
Since neither you nor I may live forever
Like this, I'll say the folly that has fooled us
Out of our lives was never mine, but yours.

"No, you are not alone,"
Seneca said: "I wish to God you were!
And I wish more that you had been so always,
That you might be so now. Your brother is here,
And yet he has not been here for ten years.

"And why I was so long
In seeing that it was never to be you,
Is not for you to tell me—for I know."

But Seneca's protests avail him nothing at all. In the end, Avenel smiles, insisting that "we have been / Too long familiar with our differences / To quarrel—or to change," and she sends him on his way.

IV *Influence in Longer Poems*

Leaving aside "The Book of Annandale" that Robinson began early and left uncompleted for years—and that even when complete may have been a polemic, after all, which the poet wanted Emma Shepherd Robinson to read and to agree with—the thematic pattern in "March of the Cameron Men," "Mortmain," and in "Late Summer" is repeated in a number of Robinson's longer poems. Or better, it is a fugue, its variations extended and meticulously—sometimes too meticulously—counterpointed: a woman, usually beautiful and intelligent, is much sought after, loved; but she is never quite obtainable by the man who seeks her. It is not only a consummation of the physical that he seeks, but possession: marriage, complete acceptance, communion, a fully compatible relationship that in an ideal sense could, or should, exist.

So, Roman Bartholow, in the poem of the same name, though married to Gabrielle, loses her while finding himself; but he is "born again" largely because of the help of a pseudo-psychiatrist, Penn-Raven; and Gabrielle, seduced by Penn-Raven and finding herself unable to live with either husband or lover or with herself, commits suicide. So, also, Matthias (in *Matthias at the Door*) finds that he cannot die until he is born again; and he loses his wife, Natalie, because their house was built on "infirm foundations"; he knows, after her death—and Garth's and Timberlake's —that he cannot begin to live until he has found himself. But Natalie has never been wholly his; she had married him for the comfort and security that he had to offer her.

Cavender, in the poem of that name, jealously suspecting Laramie, his wife, murders her, then long afterward spends an endless night in the home in which they had lived, conversing with her ghost and trying to discover whether his suspicions had been correct and that she had in fact been unfaithful to him. But in the end he had nothing and "was alone / Now, in a darker house than any light / Might enter while he lived." And which man possessed Agatha in *The Glory of the Nightingales*: Malory or Nightingale? In *Merlin*, Merlin loses Vivian, or gives her up, to return to Arthur's dying kingdom. In *Lancelot*, Lancelot loses Guinevere to a nunnery, seeking himself the "Light" that Galahad had seen. And in *Tristram*, the hero, caught in a love never to be fulfilled, loses both love and life. Joyous Guard may well have been the familiar Robinson and Shepherd property, there on the Maine coast, the rugged lines of which were in the poet's mind when he thought of Tintagel in Cornwall.[11]

These are necessary but perilous oversimplifications of the fugue theme, to be sure. But the theme nevertheless cuts obliquely through a great body of Robinson's poetry. Somehow, we are convinced, it derives from a critical moment—and a serious relationship—in the poet's life and is so repeated as to make us think he was obsessed by it.[12] Indeed, the fact that it is central even in his latest poems seems to confirm this position. Perhaps the obsession accounts for the deeply involved meanings in nearly all the long narrative poems after *Tristram* and for Malcolm Cowley's comment that they "are like the conversations of ghosts in unfurnished rooms."[13]

V *Brothers and Self*

By all accounts, Robinson had great affection for his oldest brother, Dean. "How Annandale Went Out" is unquestionably a fictional representation of the manner in which Dean died. Professor Nivison, who has already treated the poem fully, notes that "'How Annandale Went Out' is, like 'Cortege,' so important to the poet that it was almost a part of his being, to be guarded as though it were a piece of himself." The meaning of the sonnet is of course quite clear as is the problem of euthanasia with which it deals sympathetically. On the surface, the poem is simply the story of how a physician treats a patient who is "A wreck, with hell between him and the end." But, as Professor Nivison asserts, ". . . we are poorer if we are unable to consider what this poem meant to Robinson, its intimate connection with a painful memory, a case in his own life and family of that problem which always absorbed him, of worth in apparent failure, of the man enduring through the ruin."[14]

Those who regard this sonnet as contrived will find it more intensely moving when they become aware of what drove the poet to write it; for, as Professor Nivison continues in his essay, "at the level to which criticism must rise in Robinson we deal with more than just the poem; we deal with the poet as well. Criticism is more than just an esthetic-semantic problem having to do with words, and with meanings which are attributes of words—it become a moral problem of judging attitudes, which are the attributes of a man."[15]

In the Edwin-Emma-Herman relationship, however, rivalry apparently developed into jealousy. The depth of the poet's involvement is revealed in "Cortege," as has been said. To what extent that rivalry-jealousy pattern was subliminal is hard to say; but not, by any means, was all of it so. Significantly, Edwin wrote to Harry DeForest Smith as early as March 11, 1894, betraying a conscious awareness of the conflict that continued: "Your third belated letter came Saturday, and I was glad to hear that you are coming home in a fortnight. You say that your time will be pretty well taken up, but you may be willing to take one or two brief vacations and listen to my five wild sketches—not including 'Marshall.' I have another in my mind on *the philosophical enmity of two brothers who were not born for the same purpose.*"[16] [italics added]

In any case, knowing that the rivalry existed makes it easier to hear the bitter overtones in poems that seem indubitably to be portraits of Herman Robinson. "Richard Cory" comes first to mind because it is a nearly perfect representation of Edwin's next older brother; but, since this poem was written early, it may have been merely a well-imagined projection of things to come

or of things Robinson had observed. "Bewick Finzer," "Bokardo,"
and "Flammonde," however, are, as the *Memoir* suggests, among
the poems closely associated with Herman.

Cory, rich, "imperially slim," perfectly schooled in all the
amenities, the most admired man in Tilbury Town, went home
one day and "put a bullet through his head." Manifestly, Herman
took the slower, more measured, course of drink; but the result
was the same, almost as though he sought death. How much more
sharply the irony penetrates, though, if we know about the
myth! It is double-edged.

Awareness of Herman's deterioration likewise intensifies the
tragic aspect of "Bewick Finzer," probably because Finzer, far
more than Cory, is both contemporaneous and universal. Here is
a man who once had succeeded in making a fortune but who,
through a lust for more, lost everything: "And something
crumbled in his brain / When his half million went." Thereafter
he tries manfully, even in a "coat worn out with care," to keep
up appearances. Now he borrows, and "We give and then
forget." There is nothing enigmatic about Finzer: he stands like
a monument to failure, "Familiar as an old mistake / And futile
as regret," a subject of pity, or of contempt, which so often has
its roots in pity.

Similarly, in "Bokardo," the story of a man who once had
everything but who, through questionable practices, has fallen
in the world, Robinson's apparent bitterness about Herman over-
came him. Still, unless we have some knowledge of the myth,
this strange poem in many ways defies full understanding. Too
many fragments of meaning, abstractly referred, if referred at all,
lie scattered and unrelated in it.

> Talk a little; or, if not,
>   Show me with a sign
> Why it was that you forgot
>   What was yours and mine.

These are lines that suggest both anger and resentment. We are
forced to conclude that either they give expression to the poet's
condemnation of Herman's failure in the management of the
family finances, or that they represent some sharp words exchanged during a personal quarrel. In any case, the poem continues in unrelieved irony of the sharpest kind:

Friends, I gather, are small things
In an age when coins are kings;
Even at that, one hardly flings
    Friends before swine.

Rather strong? I knew as much,
    For it made you speak.
No offense to swine, as such,
    But why this hide and seek?

You have something on your side
And you wish you might have died,
So you tell me. And you tried
    One night last week?

Learn a little to forget
    Life was once a feast;
You aren't fit for dying yet,
    So don't be a beast.

Talk of debt and remorse and of decency, of time for Bokardo
to rearrange his life, suggests a period in Herman's life after his
separation from Emma when he was living a quite irregular
existence. However, the tie between Bokardo and Finzer is close
enough, though the former expresses a greater intensity of personal emotion, while the latter edges into pathos.

That Robinson in his later years yielded to a far more com-
passionate mood regarding Herman is evident in two other
short poems. "Exit," for example, might pass unnoticed as a
poem related to the myth; the *Memoir* unequivocally relates it
to Herman:

For what we owe to other days,
Before we poisoned him with praise,
May we who shrank to find him weak
Remember that he cannot speak.

For envy that we may recall,
And for our faith before the fall,
May we who are alive be slow
To tell what we shall never know.

For penance he would not confess,
And for the fateful emptiness
Of early triumph undermined,
May we now venture to be kind.

Obviously this poem is both personal and universal in its implications; yet it seems precisely to fit Herman's case, the key lines being "May we who shrank to find him weak," and "Of early triumph undermined."

"Flammonde," one of Robinson's favorite poems, relates both to "Richard Cory" and to "Bewick Finzer." Certain of its key lines become a repeated pattern:

> With news of nations in his talk
> And something royal in his walk,
> With glint of iron in his eyes,
> But never doubt, nor yet surprise,
> Appeared, and stayed, and held his head
> As one by kings accredited.

These, of course, recall Cory. Finzer reappears in such lines as

> And what he needed for his fee
> To live, he borrowed graciously.

or in

> He never told us what he was,
> Or what mischance, or other cause,
> Had banished him for better days
> To play the Prince of Castaways.

Cory comes to mind again in the lines

> His mien distinguished any crowd,
> His credit strengthened when he bowed;
> And women, young and old, were fond
> Of looking at the man Flammonde.

Surely if these poems concern Herman—and they seem to—it appears that Robinson's own experience had softened his attitude toward his brother. In analyzing his brother's character, he may have seen clearly at last that Herman possessed genius but had lacked only the propitious moment to produce unqualified success. Indeed, but for the depression, Herman might have brought a fortune to the family. That so young a man could be trusted with so much responsibility is evidence enough that his older banker colleagues respected him. Moreover, though too late to save himself, Herman broke resolutely from his drinking habits. Thus the poet wrote as if to place the blame for Herman's failures upon circumstances beyond his control: "What broken link / With-

held him from the destinies / That came so near to being his?"
Nostalgically, Robinson reminded himself:

> We cannot know how much we learn
> From those who never will return,
> Until a flash of unforeseen
> Remembrance falls on what has been.
> We've each a darkening hill to climb;
> And this is why, from time to time
> In Tilbury Town, we look beyond
> Horizons for the man Flammonde.

If Herman is here, he is praised, acknowledged, understood, mourned as, all things considered, he should be. But the poem rises far above the merely personal even though it may have been Robinson's way of giving his final approval of Herman as a man. Flammonde could have been, could be, many men, just as Finzer might be. The veiled suggestion of Flammonde as a Christ figure somehow emerges, moreover, as we analyze the name "Flammonde." For if Robinson intended to compound the two French nouns "flamme" and "monde," arranging them in a syncopated form, the word could mean "light of the world," or Christ. Robinson was an inveterate player with words and names.[17]

But the dark hill to climb, one of the poet's often used symbols, as Professor Egbert Oliver has noted, had become fixed in his mind by the time he wrote this poem—one of the numerous contrasting images of light and dark to be found in his poems, both short and long.[18] The image implies the human—Robinson's own dark hills to climb—and the corporeal at the same time that it suggests Christ on his way to Calvary.

"Annandale Again," thought to be another view of Herman in the myth but possibly portraying all three brothers from time to time, Professor Nivison has treated much as he has treated the two other Annandale poems—as reflecting an aspect of Robinson's personal history. Suffice it to say that the poems examined establish a pattern which Robinson was to employ throughout his poetic career: the failure. And, again, Robinson has played all the variations of the theme. One is a figure who seemingly has everything yet, like Cory, finds some intrinsic value missing in his life and so destroys himself. Whatever worms are eating him out, Robinson does not say and lets the reader decide. A second is a man like Finzer who once had achieved wealth and eminence and has failed. Yet he seeks to maintain an image of opulence, an acceptance in the community, by virtue of a warm personality and by sponging from friends and neighbors who tolerate him because of what he has been. Another is a man who has reached for something beyond his grasp, falling short of success or, like Palissy, like Edwin Robinson himself, sacrificing everything else in his struggle. In many of these figures is a facet of character to be admired: Captain Craig, Fernando Nash, Flammonde, even Nightingale—all are worthy in one way or another. But all are victims, as it were, of some cosmic joke: "As flies to wanton boys are we to the gods, / They kill us for their sport."

Robinson early confronted the problem of failure in himself as well as in others of his own family. His extension of the problem in so many of his creations was not, however, an intended exploitation of the subject. He wished to understand it, to probe it. Doubtless he would have preferred talking about it; but as talk was not easy for him—and he grew increasingly taciturn through the years—he wrote it out in poetic form. Indeed, writing became for him an almost compulsive substitute for speech. Nevertheless, if he in fact consciously or unconsciously used personal history, he cleverly disguised his characters and figmented situations and relationships in those poems that derived from his personal experience in order to hide their immediate identity. The reader therefore sometimes runs into allusions so private as to obscure the poet's meaning. But few, if any, of Robinson's poems fail as art, despite their occasional obscurity.

Moreover, even those poems most clearly identified with the myth, with personal history, often transcend the strictly individual and personal life of the character described. In "Miniver Cheevy," without question a self-portrait, Robinson could laugh at the contradictions in his own life; but, while laughing, he could see that Miniver was a character to be projected into the universal. If he held the glass before his eyes and saw through himself, that was one thing and was important because it gave the poem substance and a *sense* of the real. But Robinson was acutely aware of the complex and highly structured nature of poetry; and he was, moreover, too skillful a craftsman not to insist upon excellence in poetic form. Further still, he was especially conscious of the quality of language, the variable responses that words can and do elicit. In Cheevy, juxtaposed contrasts of past and present, of ideality and reality, of contempt for money and a recognized need for it, of Art and Romance on the one hand and vagrancy on the other: these are the elements that lift the poem onto a high plane of artistic achievement. Language and structure agree perfectly; and, as Robert Frost once noted, that fourth "thought" in the last line of the seventh stanza, lying in wait for the reader just around the corner of the preceding line, is a crashing crescendo of the irony infused into the whole poem.

Another poem, "Aunt Imogen," thought to be a self-portrait, is submerged in the personal yet rises far above it. Again Robinson disguised his characters, metamorphosing himself into an aunt instead of an uncle, and making delightful changelings of two of his nieces who become Sylvester and Young George. When Edwin escaped New York to visit Emma and her children, it was indeed as though he had "got away again / From cabs and clattered asphalt for a while." And he could make both the mother and the children laugh, yet, while laughing, "covering, like a scar. . . . That hungering incompleteness and regret—That passionate ache for something" of his own. For Robinson, if there had once been dreams of a life with a woman he loved—and children of his own—"There were no dreams, / No phantoms" in his future now.

> One clinching revelation of what was
> One by-flash of irrevocable chance,
> Had acridly but honestly foretold
> The mystical fulfilment of a life
> That might have once. . . . But that was all gone by:
> There was no need of reaching back for that. . . .

And yet, he could project his private sadness over what might have been into the loneliness and need of thousands of unmarried, childless, yearning Aunt Imogens. The poem is too searingly alive to be called sentimental: the paradox of the deeply human and corporeal on the one hand—

> The language, or the tone, or something else—
> Gripped like insidious fingers on her throat,
> And then went foraging af if to make
> A plaything of her heart.

and barrenness on the other.

Robinson understood well enough what he was doing: he recognized what was personal in the poem and indeed created it out of his own experience. He had years earlier written Arthur Gledhill, "'The Night Before' is an attempt to be absolutely impersonal—which, of course, is an impossiblity."[19] Yet he was able to perceive clearly that point at which the microcosmic extends into the macrocosmic.

At any rate, a list of poems that relate to the myth is far too long for consideration and exploration here. In varying degrees of involvement, the reader may find Robinson, his brothers Herman and Dean, and Emma Shepherd appearing as shadowy and disguised characters in many of the longer poems. Exactly to assess the value of that myth is not possible. The members of the Robinson family know what they know, and they doubtless know more than they now wish to reveal. But we cannot simply dismiss the biographical, for it intrudes. We should not say that a poet *must* write biography or autobiography in poetic form; it is simply that, *as* he cannot write in a vacuum, he may unconsciously—perhaps consciously—reveal himself, his society, his relationships, his entire intellectual, emotional, and psychological development in the lines that he pens over the years. So, the more we know of the poet's life, the more clearly we may be able to make meaningful what the poet has written.

CHAPTER 4

Of Lost Imperial Music

OF THE NEARLY fifteen hundred pages in Robinson's *Collected Poems*, about two hundred contain all the short poems; and the remaining thirteen hundred are devoted to the longer narratives in blank verse (sometimes regarded as poetic novels), along with some others, such as "Demos and Dionysus," that are dramatic in form. Readers and critics agree rather generally that the poet's reputation rests on the shorter poems but some notable exceptions are made. The poems most familiar to readers today are those usually found in anthologies of American poetry, the longest of which is the always popular "Ben Jonson Entertains a Man from Stratford." This customary anthologizing doubtless contributes to the general preference for and the familiarity with the shorter poems. But whether the long narratives deserve the kind of library-shelf oblivion to which they have in recent years been consigned is open to question. Today, unfortunately, they are brought out for reading chiefly by graduate students in American literature seminars—if they are removed from the shelf at all.

Sometimes Robinson is charged with being repetitious in his themes and narrow in his range of subject matter, but other poets have been indicted for the same weaknesses. These are easy critical comments to make; for any poet's style, his manner of phrasing, his vocabulary, his tricks of language, may give rise to such views to the hasty reader or to one surfeiting himself with too much of the poet's work at one time. To read the greater part of Robinson's poetic canon over the years is to discover, however, that this charge against him is oversimplified.

I *Nature*

The fact that Robinson's chief concern is with the human equation in all its complexities made it inevitable that he would range widely and with infinite variety in the subjects of his poems. For all his disdain of tinkling water and red-bellied robins, for example, he saw much in nature to utilize as a backdrop for a human situation. In "Isaac and Archibald" the sunlit country-side appears at frequent intervals:

> . . . and the world
> Was wide, and there was gladness everywhere.
> We walked together down the River Road
> With all the warmth and wonder of the land
> Around us, and the wayside flash of leaves,—
> And Isaac said the day was glorious. . . .

Farther in the same poem one finds another bright passage:

> . . . and I felt
> Within the mightiness of the white sun
> That smote the land around us and wrought out
> A fragrance from the trees, a vital warmth
> And fullness for the time that was to come,
> And a glory for the world beyond the forest.

These are not isolated instances. "Two Gardens in Linndale" contain some sure, deft strokes:

> He sees the ghost of gentle Oakes
> Uprooting, with a restless hand,
> Soft, shadowy flowers in a land
> Of asphodels and artichokes.

The poignant images in one of Robinson's many carefully wrought sonnets, "The Sheaves," reflect the poet's perceptive eye:

> Where long the shadows of the wind had rolled,
> Green wheat was yielding to the change assigned;
> And as by some vast magic undivined
> The world was turning slowly into gold.
> Like nothing that was ever bought or sold
> It waited there, the body and the mind;
> And with a mighty meaning of a kind
> That tells the more the more it is not told.

The last four lines of the sestet are some of Robinson's most remarkable and colorful:

> A thousand golden sheaves were lying there,
> Shining and still, but not for long to stay—
> As if a thousand girls with golden hair
> Might rise from where they slept and go away.

In *Merlin* he used, among other natural images, the very words that he had earlier dismissed from his poetic credo: tinkling water! He speaks of "rays of broken sunshine," of a "fountain raining crystal music," of "all the green / Around the tinkling fountain where she gazed / Upon the circling pool. . . ." Indeed, nature is the idyllic background for Merlin and Vivian in Broceliande.

II *Man*

But man, not nature, is Robinson's central concern: man's vicissitudes, his labor, his joy and sorrow, his hope and ambition, his despair, and even his defeat. From the inconsequential anonymity of his "Doctor" of billiards to that Atlas among men, Fernando Nash, in whose listening dream a great symphony is played to save the dreamer from death—for a time at least; from Lancelot, the great hero of Arthur's court, lover of Guinevere, seeker after the "Light," to Eben Flood, with his precious remembering jug, looking back at a town housed by ghosts and once-opened doors—lost, alone—all were nourished and most of them grew to full stature in the poet's active imagination.

The temptation to classify all the works of an author always rises invitingly into the mind of a literary critic. For classification may, and sometimes does, bring into focus the artist's dominant themes, patterns, and subjects. The danger inherent in categorizing is that readers (including students) are inclined to substitute category for close reading and critical analysis. In his complexity and diversity Robinson does not lend himself readily to that kind of cubbyholing whereof the reader can take comfort and assurance.[1] Robinson's inclination to regard every man as a distinct individual mitigates against it.

Nevertheless, themes and patterns and subjects do emerge from Robinson's poetry. Not all, by any means, either can or need be examined in this brief study; and only the most evident of them, broadly defined, are noted here. How the themes of the meticulously compressed short poems are sometimes repeated and extended in the more leisurely pace of the long narratives is also noticed.

III *Failure*

We have already seen, in an examination of those poems that reflect personal history, Robinson's involvement with the problem of failure in our lives. Why he devoted so many of his writing hours to this subject is not easily explained. Possibly he was motivated by his own failure to achieve recognition that he sought, a feeling that persisted in him for many frustrated years. Unquestionably, he was moved deeply by the tragic incidence of failure in the lives of his two brothers. It is apparent, however, that man as failure became for him a part of his cosmic view of the world he lived in. Perhaps the "why" was as inexplicable to him as the mystery of life itself. *How* he treated his failure-figure, whose faces peered over the edge of his writing table, sometimes despondently, sometimes hopefully, is of greater significance.

Broadly defined, the theme follows two patterns: one is the failure who seems to be beyond redemption, who does not, finally, possess the saving grace of character that would find favor in men's eyes, or who does not experience some inner change that would render less severe the general indictment against him. The other is the failure who for reasons of almost infinite variety is redeemed, exonerated, saved, or in whom the reader finds some aspect or some alteration of the inner man that lifts him from the shame of complete ignominy.

The first of these types is not so numerous as the second, but he is distinctly marked, even then. While in another relationship Richard Cory was considered in the preceding chapter, he falls into the general class of the failure; and the poem in which he is the central figure lives because it is a powerful statement of an inner, even if an undefined, tragedy in the life of one man. The external man the "people on the pavement" praised and envied and acknowledged; for Cory, to them, seemingly had everything. What private sense of failure, what personal recognition of his own inadequacy, or what secret unfulfilled longing drove Cory to suicide Robinson does not say; he leaves the reason for his readers to determine. But the crashing climactic moment of the night that Richard Cory "went home and put a bullet through his head" appalls every reader with its suddenness. After he has recovered from his shock and has reflected upon the intensity of the poem created by the contrast of the somber people of the community on the one hand and the brilliant heroic stature of Cory on the other, the reader is left with a sharp sense of emptiness, of a life wasted, of failure— and of Cory's hidden agony.

Wasted, too, is the life of Robinson's "Doctor" of billiards who is the "last" of "all among the fallen from on high," who clicks away his kingdom with "three spheres of insidious ivory," and who exchanges his crown for "cap and bells." His is a not uncommon type of failure, the man without direction or purpose, unredeemed by any of the saving graces. In "Miniver Cheevy" Robinson portrays with wry irony a chap who misses, and complains about missing, all the beauty and all the glorious evil of the past. Paradoxically, the reader smiles and is sad; for Miniver is a humorous figure and at the same time one to be pitied. Unredeemed and unredeemable, Cheevy scratches his head and coughs; he keeps on swigging his liquor and sinks into a comfortable oblivion. But Robinson's Aaron Stark is the most severely treated of these three. Far more meager than Miniver, Aaron is a miser, "Cursed and unkempt, shrewd, shrivelled, and morose" whose words fall on his listeners like "sullen blows / Through scattered fangs . . .," and who laughs at those few who can find some pity in their hearts for him. Utterly damned and beyond saving, he is even beyond wishing to be saved!

The central figure of "Tasker Norcross" is, among Robinson's hollow men, perhaps the most likely to have some claim on our sympathies; for he is aware of his emptiness—or Ferguson is; and Ferguson, we learn, *is* Tasker Norcross. In this poem Robinson has once again arranged a dialogue between himself (the first-person, minor-character viewpoint) and another person. The device of having Ferguson talk about Tasker as a third character is unusual in the poet's work, but the poem is not therefore obscure or even confusing. As the fiction is begun, Ferguson describes three kinds of people who live in his town: the good, the not so good, and Tasker Norcross. Now, he says, there are only two kinds. His listener replies: "Meaning, as I divine, /

Your friend is dead. . . ." When Ferguson answers "My friends are dead— / Or most of them," his identity is established.

We might find the locale of the poem in Gardiner: "An old house, painted white, / Square as a box, and chillier than a tomb / To look at or to live in." There are almost too many trees in front of it and around it. And "Down in front / There was a road, a railroad, and a river; / Then there were hills behind it, and more trees." Ethan Frome might have lived there, or Aaron Stark; but it is Tasker Norcross who has lived there with a houseful of old ghosts of ancestors, each of whom had lived and died with his honor. Norcross lives there, being neither good nor bad—nor anything, for that matter—with his illusions in "his tethered range." He listens to great music, but it does not reach or stir him. His house and garden are filled with fine art pieces, but he can see neither their beauty nor their living quality. He knows that the world turns and is full of people whose voices he hears but whose words have no meaning for him, who "would have served and honored him, / And saved him, had there been anything to save." When he died nobody mourned; and when the house was up for auction, a stranger bought it. But it was Ferguson's house that he bought and lived in and was never warm in. When questioned, the stranger admits to having known Ferguson "as a man may know a tree—" but neither he nor anyone else had ever heard of Tasker Norcross. Self-knowledge is not, in Tasker's case, enough. He holds himself "a little high," too high for seeing how high he might have seen could he have seen below him! Like Finzer and Bokardo, Tasker must have his illusions.

Such men as these are not to be redeemed, are not to experience an inner change that might save them in other men's eyes. Robinson does not condemn them; it is as though he says: "This is the way the world turns on its bent axis." But the second of his failure types fares somewhat better. Occasionally, he may even find a happier end than these other lost souls. So, in "Bon Voyage," that "child of a line accurst / And old as Troy," no matter that he wastes his life getting and giving and spending without a care—his world a "Feast or a funeral"—yet plays a "twinkling part" which is his lot in life. Perhaps it is his twinkling that the world approves and delights in that redeems him; and when that dies, he fades and dies before we are aware of his passing.

Shadrach O'Leary, poet extraordinary, who celebrates the female charms and wiles in his songs, writes pretty trash for years. The day comes, however, when he must face the moment of truth. Recognizing himself as a failure, he puts his poetry aside—apparently for an occupation that permits him to respect himself at last. For he has found the "Gleam" and is a "failure spared." Uncle Ananias, too, would be a total failure except that his prevarications have a fascination about them. Everyone understands him. Children sit at his feet, carried away by his exaggerated tales until at last he wins the "laurel of approved iniquity." And all the children love him faithfully.

In "The Growth of 'Lorraine'" the heroine also fails. Driven by physical urges over which she has no control and unwilling to accept and be content with the humdrum married life that most women seek, she tells her lover

> "I've gone too far; the life would be too slow.
> Some could have done it—some girls have the stuff;
> But I can't do it: I don't know enough.
> I'm going to the devil."—And she went.

When her lover reads her letter some years afterward, he is not surprised to learn that at length she has recognized her inability to continue as a slave of passion and has committed suicide. The title of the poem is not the "death" but the "growth" of Lorraine; in her recognition has come the need for a freedom that only death can bring to her. It is not that Robinson approved of suicide; in this case, he neither approved nor condemned. For the kind of "love" to which Lorraine becomes a slave destroys her even before she swallows the five poisonous drops; and she is redeemed by bringing an end to her tragic plight.

Robinson compressed this tragic drama cunningly within the compass of twenty-eight lines—a two-sonnet sequence. No other poet of his time matched that achievement; and few, before or since, if any at all, have succeeded so brilliantly. The sonnet is not and never has been the usual vehicle for poetic drama, but Robinson appears to have invented the technique. In the first of the two sonnets he presents an indefinite situation: the reader finds no particularized stage, no backdrop, and must imagine where Lorraine and her lover have met and at what time of day or night. The lover listens while Lorraine tells him, in the octave, about her tragic flaw: she is a slave to passion. In the sestet, she rejects, as we have seen, the conventional pattern for women in this world and goes to the devil in her own fashion. We do not *see* Lorraine or her lover. We do not know their coloring, the shapes or expressions of their faces, the tone of Lorraine's voice or its accent—nor do we need to. The situation calls for privacy; and the anonymity that Robinson achieved by his use of quotation marks around the name "Lorraine," along with a similar anonymity for the lover, makes this privacy possible. The reader uncritically accepts his audience position with the fourth wall of the "stage" open to him.

In the second sonnet, the lover appears *soli*, reading a letter, the contents of which we have already noted. The octave reveals Lorraine's remembrance of her lover—she calls him "friend"— and her decision to die. In the sestet she explains her reason— which is a kind of triumph also—for taking poison, her recognition scene in a flashback. This brevity, the amazing compression of a life story, makes this tragic spectacle so effective. The reader is left with few if any questions to ask. For an intensely painful moment in time and space he has been struck by the sharp edge of a cruel reality yet at last, like the lover, he cannot be either "surprised or grieved."

Two extensions of the failure theme are to be found in "Captain Craig" and *The Man Who Died Twice,* both classic representations of men discredited and broken by the world who nevertheless triumph because, at least in Robinson's eyes, they redeem themselves. The astounding fact is that Robinson manages to lift these shabby creatures to admirable levels, granting each a distinct individuality and convincing his reader that both have gained stature in men's esteem.

Though Alfred Hyman Louis was the archetypal pattern for his "pauper," in "Captain Craig" Robinson poured all of his own idealism, his own altruism into the old man. The locus of the poem is spare enough: a bed and one chair in an unadorned room fit only for a castaway. Again, as in "Lorraine," the reader has almost nothing of the physical image of Craig; the hands appear and are felt, along with the penetrating eyes that on occasion glimmer wearily. But these are negligible matters; it is the cerebration that counts. Seemingly coming from out of nowhere, a failure even at panhandling, Craig is full of the world's wisdom that he shares with the six young men who have discovered him in Tilbury Town.

Probably not ten people had ever shaken Craig's hand. He sang a song out of harmony with the general chant and so was ignored. The citizens of Tilbury ". . . . might have made him sing by feeding him / Till he should march again," but

> They found it more melodious to shout
> Right on, with unmolested adoration,
> To keep the tune as it had always been,
> To trust in God, and let the Captain starve.

To Robinson, such is always the destiny of the iconoclast. Craig has failed, but as the young men listen to him, they are singularly struck by him and by what he says:

> But soon there came assurance of his lips,
> Like phrases out of some sweet instrument
> Man's hand had never fitted, that he felt
> "No penitential shame for what had come,
> Nor virtuous regret for what had been,—
> But rather a joy to find it in his life
> To be an outcast usher of the soul
> For such as had good courage of the Sun
> To pattern Love."

Not all the six young men sit at the master's feet to share his wisdom, however. Robinson cleverly projects himself in the role of first-person, minor character in this fiction. The "I" in the poem is thus early established as the point of view, and the other young companions come onto the scene only briefly from time to time. In addition, Robinson employs the letter device in a portion of this poem. Absenting himself (the "I") from Tilbury for a period of about six months, he receives long epistles from his old friend and thereby is permitted to give his reader the full texture of the Captain's mind. The structure of the poem, however, is arranged in a simple chronological progression—in this case, a kind of slice-of-life technique: beginning with the "discovery" of the Captain by Robinson (the "I"), Killigrew, Carmichael, and the others, and ending with Craig's death and funeral.

So much for the framework of the poem. Craig, a failure in the deadly measuring eyes of Tilbury folk, fascinates the reader by virtue of his erudition—and his nonsense; by the largeness of his humor; and by his refusal meekly to accept defeat, to submit to despair. Manifestly he reflects the young Robinson who found joy both in discovering his pauper and in writing about him. What is more intriguing, Robinson seems to say, than to find an old man with young ideas, unsoured by the dark world? Craig is such a man, or he is any man we please; and the reader may dip into the poem again and again, putting his finger on a passage and saying: "Now this is exactly the way I look at life and wish to think about it." Craig is a man to heed. "The world that has been old is young again," he says;

> "The touch that faltered clings; and this is May.
> So think of your decrepit pensioner
> As one who cherishes the living light,
> Forgetful of dead shadows."

Out of this mood, suddenly, a Wordsworthian fancy comes:

> "Think first of him as one who vegetates
> In tune with all the children who laugh best
> And longest through the sunshine, though far off
> Their laughter, and unheard; for't is the child,
> O friend, that with his laugh redeems the man."

Then, as suddenly, Craig stabs at man in the general:

> "We men, we shearers of the Golden Fleece—
> Were brutes without him,—brutes to tear the scars
> Of one another's wounds and weep in them,
> And then cry out on God that he should flaunt
> For life such anguish and flesh-wretchedness.
> But let the brute go roaring his own way:
> We do not need him, and he loves us not."

Some of these lines reflect Craig in his varying moods. He is not always gay, as we have seen earlier in his words about the debutante. He listens to the music of the world attentively, hearing both harmony and dissonance; but he does not scramble these extremes into a finale of musical chaos. Rather, he concludes with a note, however faintly played, of hope. There was a time when he had "hounds and credit" and, as he says, "grave friends / To borrow my books and set wet glasses on them," not unlike Robinson's old acquaintance, Alfred Louis. But if he has become a failure and a castaway, the veritable prince of his defunct tribe in the eyes of the materialist, Craig has not lost all savor of life. Even as he lies on his bed, facing death and the young men who are visiting him, he belabors them for their fear of life, of living. For "if it be fear," he says to them, "then I can do no more / Than hope for all of you that you may find / Your promise of the sun. . . ." If it were grief, he challenges them, then why had they taken his words "For more than ever misers did their gold?" His last spoken word, "Trombones" is a cry to life from the shadow of death. Trombones in the Tilbury band that will play, in his funeral procession, the "Dead March" from *Saul!* Enough, surely, to redeem him, to reveal him as worthy!

The story of Fernando Nash of *The Man Who Died Twice*, Robinson devised in quite another manner and with quite another figure. If "Craig" wanders in structure (though not irrelevantly) just as the loquacious Captain wanders with oddments of ideas, *The Man Who Died Twice* concentrates undeviatingly upon its hero. Again Robinson establishes the "I," the first-person minor-character viewpoint, in order to give verisimilitude to the fiction. He begins his narrative almost at the point where Nash's life has ended, thereafter flashing backward in an extended explication of Fernando's fall from greatness. Robinson employs, besides, and with superb skill, the device of a mirror that permits Nash to reveal himself to himself and to the reader at the same time:

> . . . he sat before a glass
> That was more like a round malevolent eye
> Filmed with too many derelict reflections,
> Appraising there a bleared and heavy face
> Where sodden evil should have been a stranger.

> "What are you doing here? And who are you?"

he queries himself, as if at the beginning of a cross-examination. And at the end of his soliloquy of self-examination and self-recrimination, he concludes:

> Look at Fernando Nash,—
> The heir-apparent of a throne that's ashes,
> The king who lost his crown before he had it,
> And saw it melt in hell."

Fernando Nash dies twice before he dies. He "had it" once: the genius for musical composition, an "upstanding Ajax" of a man; and all he had to do was wait for those "celestial messengers" to bring to his creative ear "that great golden choral fire of sound" which would become a symphony for the ages. He could not wait; he became instead for twenty years a "paramount whale of lust and drunkenness," a failure. As an artist, he dies— his first death. But it is not his finding the glory of God that saves him, nor is it the beating of a drum for a group of street-singing evangelists. For all his allegiance to the Lord is only an "earnest of thanksgiving," or it may have been "confusion, penance, or the picturesque." At last he hears, above the drums, "that choral golden overflow / Of sound and fire. . . ." that in his mind's ear he has always heard yet has not "heard before." What he has waited for has come, finally, to redeem him; and he cannot wait but staggers out of his room to find a score on which to set the music down. Too late!

> Crying aloud to God, a man, or devil,
> For paper—not for food. It may have been
> The devil who heard him first and made of him,
> For sport, the large and sprawling obstacle
> They found there at the bottom of the stairs.

Following this climactic passage, which is a momentous crescendo, Nash's life symphony closes—pianissimo. What he had once, he has found again; and though he cannot preserve it on a score, he has to his own satisfaction and elation—and convincingly to the reader's as well—grasped finally the greatness that he has never truly lost.

In *The Man Who Died Twice*, we see Robinson's finest development of the failure-redeemed theme, not only because of its well-framed structure but also because of the poet's masterful use of the language of music—not the compositional terms alone, though there are these: "This innovation of orchestral rats," "A most arbitrary intermezzo," the "sordid prelude," "the infernal fugue." The poetic imagery sings in a more melodious key than we hear pitched in most of Robinson's blank-verse narratives. Alliterations are more prominent: "And scorn for power, and hell for paradise"; "They soiled with earthy feet the shining floor / Flinging the dregs of their debaucheries"; "They shrieked and sang in shrill delirium"; "By a rich idiot, and insanely sunk / In darker water than where ships go down"; Take me somewhere to sea and let me sink / And fear not for my soul. / I have found that."

The music imagery is especially rich. Nash's genius is a thing "Blown down by choral horns out of a star / To quench those drums of death with singing fire / Unfelt by man before."; "Still muffled within the same unyielding cloud / Of sound and fire, which had somewhere within it / A singing flame that he might not for long / Endure. . . ."; "A lean and slinking mute with a bassoon, / Who seized attention when a languid hush / Betrayed a perilous rift of weariness / Where pleasure was not joy, and blew a tune / Of hollow triumph on a chilly reed / From which all shrank." Even to a man with one deaf ear, a bassoon can at times become a "chilly reed."

But these are only a few of the parts of what we might call a musical whole: an orchestration of compressed simplicity.[2] Indeed, the meticulous structuring of this poem, its order and unity, its flow of beauty in language, and its intense emotional impact make it one of the most outstanding of Robinson's poetic achievements. As Lewis M. Isaacs, a close friend of Robinson for many years, wrote pertinently: "Like the thematic material in a symphony, phrases, 'musical mottoes,' and the images they evoke are repeated and developed at length in a manner which may fairly be described as symphonic. You seem to hear the changes in mood and tempo from episode to episode; the gathering of force of the main themes; the climax and the great finale. And always—as in a fine musical work—you have the sense of beauty in structure as well as in sound."[3]

Something of Robinson's own life and spirit informs this narrative. For one thing, he had sufficient understanding and appreciation of music to be knowledgeable about its uses in a poetic framework. He was acutely sensitive to sound, despite his one bad ear, and he unquestionably "heard" a line of poetry as he read it to himself. He wrote once to Arthur Nevin: "I find it rather difficult to say anything tangible or satisfactory about the relation of music and poetry—music being poetry and poetry being music. . . . Generally speaking, I should be inclined to say that the field of poetry is infinitely more various and less definable than that of music, for the simple reason that poetry is language and music at the same time. . . ."[4] Perhaps his view helps to account for the many lyrical passages that we find in such long narratives as *Merlin* and *Tristram*, two among a number of poems in which the cadence and the word-sound of music can be heard.

For another thing, Robinson may easily have reflected, in the anguished, desperate years of Fernando Nash's life, upon his own bitter experience, denied as he was for so long any recognition at all for honest and competent—indeed, significantly artistic—craftsmanship. Nor could he have been unmindful (even as he portrayed in such soul-wrenching terms the debauch of his giant) of his own dark years when alcohol alone eased the pain of despair and frustration. But however the personal experience intruded, Robinson was always consciously an artist, and the artistry in this portrait of a failure redeemed is everywhere apparent. He found always in Nash

> A giant's privacy of lone communion
> With older giants who made a music
> Whereof the world was not impossibly
> Not the last note. . . .

Then, too,

> . . . there was in him always,
> Unqualified by guile and unsubdued
> By failure and remorse, or by redemption,
> The grim nostalgic passion of the great
> For glory all but theirs."

So the poet could believe in this giant, much as he had believed in himself—enough at least to keep the "machine" going:

> Crippled or cursed or crucified, the giant
> Was always there, and always will be there.

> I believe him
> Today as I believed him while he died,
> And while I sank his ashes in the sea.

Consciously, then, Robinson was aware of himself, of his earlier struggles; his own life he invested and projected in the character of Fernando Nash. The commingling brought to fruition a poem of passionate beauty and consummate power.

IV *Amaranth*

Robinson's final word on the failure theme is in his next to last long narrative, *Amaranth.* More than twice the length of *The Man Who Died Twice,* it lacks the compression as well as the music of the shorter poem. But that is not to say that it fails in structure or in thematic force. Critics who dismiss it as merely dull, just as they dismiss a number of Robinson's late blank-verse fictions, would do well to reassess it in relation to the poet's total canon.

Amaranth is a dream allegory; in most respects this poem differs from anything that Robinson had ever attempted in his long career. It is, at the same time, a kind of summation of the failure type—a roundup of all the failure types. Again, it is an examination of individuals who are misfits in life, square pegs, living in the "wrong world." Once again, it is a commentary concerned with self-deception, self-delusion, of the individual who cannot accommodate himself to his society because, simply put, he cannot or will not face reality—the truth about himself. As we read the poem we find a legion of Robinson's figures rushing back into our minds: men and women who have somehow failed, dreamed a wrong dream, lived in an unreal world. This poem gives the impression that the poet had seen a light more glaring and revealing than any he had seen before, and that he must now cast its penetrating rays across the field of folk that he has gathered together for the occasion of this poetic fiction! All of them, no doubt, he had seen at Peterborough.

Fargo, the hero of the tale, is forty-five. As a young man, he had thought of himself as an artistic genius, and for years he had labored zealously with brush and pallette and easel, convinced that his work was rare. But at thirty-five, facing the truth like Shadrach O'Leary, he decided that whatever genius he possessed was not enough and gave up art for the manufacture of water pumps. He therefore made a bonfire of his paintings— all but one; and as the poem opens he has wakened, content with life, "cleansed and cured" of his misguided, wrongheaded ambition. Yet in his room as he lies half awake

> With a sleepy glance
> At his accusing remnant on the wall,
> He rubbed his eyes, and thought. It was not bad;
> It was about as good as a few thousand
> That hands no worse than his would do somewhere
> Before the day was over.

And then he falls asleep again and dreams. And in his dream he finds himself in a world that he has seen once before. There he meets Amaranth (Truth-Reality).

> If it was man, it might have been all men
> And women there as one. All who have been,

> And all alive and all unborn were there
> Before him, and their eyes were watching him
> Out of those two that might have been the eyes
> Of death, if death were life.

What Fargo is soon to learn in full, Amaranth tells him in brief:

> But since you have come back to me,
> To the wrong world whence I delivered you,
> Now you shall see. For those who damn themselves
> By coming back, voices are not enough.
> They must have ears and eyes to know for certain
> Where they have come, and to what punishment.

From that point on, Fargo must follow Amaranth through a world that spins in space somewhere between the real and the unreal, between dream and workaday reality. But because the reader knows that Fargo is dreaming, he accepts the fantasy; and because he accepts the fantasy—activating a set of circumstances in the unconscious mind as convincing as a dream often is—whatever Robinson presents becomes fantastically real. Thus, meeting Evensong, the flutist, Pink, the poet, Atlas, the stevedore-artist, Figg, the lawyer, Styx, the physician, Flax, the clergyman, and Elaine Amelia Watchman, who writes and writes, and Amperes, her cat—we find a queer cross-section of people who have chosen to achieve success in occupations for which they have no talent. Some who face Amaranth (Truth-Reality) and look into his eyes, like Pink and Amelia Watchman, die or commit suicide. Others, like Styx, Evensong, Figg, and Flax remain alive; but each one recognizes the role of failure that he must accept as his part to play in life's dark drama. Enough to say that Fargo inevitably wakens, gradually, into the "right world where he had learned to know / That he was living there, and was not dying / Of slow deceit. . . ." Inexplicably, however, he has gone back to the wrong world and now is chastened by his dream experience.

Pondering the fantasy, the reader can only ask "Why?" And whatever answers can be given are as unsatisfying and as incomplete as they would be if the question had been asked about the meaning of life and death. Possibly Robinson had no decisive answers, or possibly he did not believe that there were any. It had long been his habit simply to present a complex situation without judging or completely explaining those involved in it. Yet we notice in *Amaranth* that, except for Ipswich, his characters are almost exclusively would-be artists and professional people: people of the kind that he had been most closely associated with at Peterborough. We learn what happens to each figure. An examination of the poem with these limits in mind may bring some of its meaning into clearer focus.

Certainly for Robinson a search for truth—or reality—was of great importance. He had stated this position even as early as his composition of "Captain Craig." If in his youthful exuberance he asserted to Harry DeForest Smith that he was an idealist, his idealism altered before long to become a "desperate optimism." And a close reading of his many letters through the years reveals that even this desperate optimism faded, for he accepted the fact that an ideal world could be no more than an illusion. Yet, illusion or reality, he insisted that the individual must search for the truth about himself and face it. In essence, *Amaranth* is a poem concerned with what happens to people who face the truth about themselves.

Lawyer Figg sums up his case, which is pretty much that for Styx and Flax. "What you behold," he says to Amaranth,

> Is not ourselves, but whims and caricatures
> Of our mishandled heritage. We may say,
> And with no unsubstantial arrogance,
> Or thin defense of our lost usefulness,
> That in the proper light of our beginning
> We shone for more than this. And as we are,
> There may be more of us than we reveal;
> We make a tinkling jest of the wrong road
> That brought us here, but when we are alone
> We put the bells away.

Figg, Styx, and Flax—all failures by any reasonable measure of men's work—will yet go on, deluded, accepting their mediocrity, defensively admitting that they took the wrong road but still unwilling squarely to face the truth.

Pink, the poet, looks into the eyes of truth and hangs himself. Elaine Amelia Watchman challenges Amaranth, looks into his eyes and, puff, becomes a small heap of dust upon the floor. Atlas empties his bottle glass by glass, looks defiantly at Amaranth, and destroys his pictures with a knife. Defiantly he accepts failure, but it is clear that he will drink himself into a morbid state of acceptance. Fargo has several opportunities to take an easier course of escape than to face the truth; but having once faced it, he has developed courage to refuse escape. Amaranth summarizes Fargo's position in this way:

> My friend, you heard me, once,
> And dared escape from here. What have you done
> To fate since then that you are here once more?
> There are men so disordered and wrong sighted,
> So blind with self, that freedom, when they have it,
> Is only a new road, and not a long one,
> To new imprisonment. But you, my brother,
> You are not one of them. You caught yourself
> Once in the coiling of a wrong ambition,
> And had the quickness to writhe out of it.
> You heard me, and you acted, and were free;
> And you are here where now there is no freedom.

No matter what the cost, Robinson seems to say, it is better to possess the truth even if the knowledge destroy the one who seeks it. In any case, an artist cannot be an artist unless he fearlessly seeks the truth about his art. Fargo has achieved peace by recognizing his lack of talent, by honestly accepting his limitations. His dream, in which he returns to and then once again escapes from the wrong world, only reinforces his belief that he had made the right choice: to shun the unreal world of self-deceit and self-delusion in which he pretended to himself that he was an artist, and to accept the reality of pump-making as his proper role in life.

Yet it would be a mistake to assume that Robinson developed any systematic body of philosophy on the subject of the individual—failure or success. He held to certain principles, among them, quite clearly, the concept that self-realization comes only with self-understanding, self-knowledge. He recognized that the world was full of failures, some lacking any saving characteristics, some redeemed and worthy in men's eyes though possessed of no world-shaking or heroic proportions. Whatever he may have thought or said privately about this man or that, in his poetry he condemned no one. He let the reader make the judgment.

Nevertheless, the artist, and particularly the poet, was a special case for Robinson. In one of his first-published sonnets he pleaded for one man to arise "To wrench one banner from the western skies, / And mark it with his name forevermore": someone who could put to flight the "little sonnet-men" who, "in a shrewd mechanic way," wrote "songs without souls." He was impatient with mediocrity, with those who refused to take infinite pains with their work, with those who rushed too quickly for the credit lines of publication. There were plainly too many, like Pink in *Amaranth,* utterly lacking in talent; and it was better by far that they not write at all than write trash. Those with ambitions who sought his advice and criticism, as has been noted, received his honest comment, even a rebuke if he thought necessary; for he believed that the artist must cling to the highest possible standards if his achievement were to have substance and the special kind of immortality that the printed page gives him.

V *Vagaries of Love*

Another broadly encompassing thematic frame in Robinson's poetry concerns the vagaries of love or sex. Patently, the subject is infinitely variable. To attempt to classify all the complex relationships between men and women is unnecessary, even if it were possible; and it involves, in any event, an unrewarding labor. Robinson saw plainly enough that men and women meet, fall in or out of love, for one reason or another find that marriage is, or is not, an arrangement that they should consider. As we have seen, he had experienced failure in his own suit for a woman's hand. He saw, too, that within the conjugal structure when conflict arises, either one or the other or both parties may be responsible. And it was inevitable that, as a subject for fiction, the triangle complication—or the threat of one—would be useful to him; for he realized that through the ages troubadours, artists, and poets have permuted it endlessly. Indeed, as sex is a significant factor in the human equation, if for no other reason, he found it a compelling matter for his poems.

Louis Untermeyer's comment that "Robinson was fascinated with other people's marital relations. . . ." was an unfortunate oversimplification—if there is any truth in the statement at all—especially since it is followed by the bitingly abbreviated "he himself never married."[5] In the light of Robinson's commitment to the human situation, marital relations do not appear to have become an obsession with him; nor does he permit himself to pronounce judgment upon his characters. Moreover, it is folly to think that, because he never married, he was unaware of the realities of sex or marriage and could not speak with an authentic voice; he knew women well enough.[6] Quite apart from the tragic circumstances involving his brother Herman and his sister-in-law, Emma Shepherd Robinson—to whatever extent he was involved with Emma and, therefore, a third party to a triangle—life in New York crowded around him in rooming houses and cheap hotels; and for years at Peterborough he was witness—as some of his letters reveal—to the inevitable romantic affairs of an artist's colony, innocent or otherwise.[7]

Yet to those today who are treated to a surfeit of sex novels, who are subjected to the intimacies of the bedroom and are immediate witnesses to love-making, both tender and violent, Robinson's development of the love theme may appear innocuous. It was not that he had no concern for the physical but that he had greater concern for the minds of his characters. If this fact makes him a poet of the cerebral and of the psychological, so be it. As a rule he shunned the direct scene of action, whether it involved sex or not. Thus in *Roman Bartholow*, we learn that Penn-Raven has seduced Gabrielle, but we do not witness the seduction. So far as that goes, this long narrative contains one of the rare scenes of physical violence to be found in Robinson's entire poetic canon. In a rage, Roman knocks Penn-Raven down; and, in turn, Penn-Raven grapples with and fells his host, pinning him helplessly in a chair.

In *Lancelot*, we know that Guinevere resents her marriage to Arthur, having had no choice in the selection of her husband. We learn that she is mistress to Arthur's most trusted knight, yet we see nothing of her private embraces with her lover. Only through Sir Lucan's report to the King do we discover how Lancelot, mad with fear and anger, has charged with his men to free the Queen from her trial-by-fire, laying about him furiously and killing, among others, two of Gawaine's brothers. After the classical fashion, it would appear, Robinson treated both violence and sex as off-stage matters.

Violence might have been accepted by his reading public. But it is doubtful that sex in its rawer forms (had he been willing to portray it) would have been any more welcome in his poetry than were the harsh implications of sex in his plays. It becomes needful, therefore, to examine his poems wherein he has treated the relationship between man and woman, both to discover his thematic intimations and to ascertain whether he has been successful in his intent.

If, as has been suggested in an earlier chapter, Robinson was motivated to write certain poems by factors relevant to his personal history, we may say that the search for an ideal woman—the always unattainable woman—was a strongly developed theme. The complex nature of the myth makes interpretation of such poems as "The March of the Cameron Men," for example, a matter of controvesy; but with or without the myth, the suitor rejected or the unattainable woman is implicitly thematic. In some of his shorter poems Robinson dealt with lovers in different ways. We are hard pressed to say whether, in "John Gorham," John or Jane Wayland is at fault for the failure of their love affair. He accuses her of playing a cat-and-mouse game with him; she replies by insisting that he simply does not try, has never tried, really to understand her: "Won't you ever see me as I am, John Gorham, / Leaving out the foolishness and all I never meant? / Somewhere in me there's a woman, if you know the way / to find her." Perhaps she has seemed to be too frivolous, has played a game too long; or perhaps John Gorham is too literal, too un-aware of feminine nature, but the moonlight that falls on them in their last meeting falls, he says, "As on two that have no longer anything to tell." John Gorham rejects Jane, and there's an end to their romance.

"Her Eyes" tells in the simplest of quatrains how an artist has given up everything in the world to achieve success in his art; and at last his work wins the plaudits of the world. But persisting through the years has been his dream of one woman whom he has loved and whom he might have married had he not "buried his days in a nameless tomb." Suddenly, he decides to create her image on his canvas and does so, making her life-like—"glowing and fair," with a perilous though angelic face. It is her eyes, at last, however, that give the figure meaning. And the quatrain that lifts the poem to the level of the truly memor-able has to do with these eyes:

> But he wrought them at last with a skill so sure
> That her eyes were the eyes of a deathless woman,—
> With a gleam of heaven to make them pure,
> And a glimmer of hell to make them human.

Like another Pygmalion, he worships her as though she were indeed his wife. Somehow, for him, she spans the long bitter struggling years between "the world that was and the world that is," perhaps between the real and the ideal. The temptation rises, of course, to regard this poem as personal history. But if so, it is essentially a projection of what Robinson imagined might be his situation at some time in the distant future, for he wrote the poem long before he had achieved fame.

Perhaps the most haunting of all the short poems on the "lost love" theme, and one of the finest of his early poems, is "Luke Havergal." Robinson himself called it his "uncomfortable abstraction"; Teddy Roosevelt liked it but confessed that he did not understand it; and many who read it today likewise confess liking the poem at the same time that they are puzzled by it. Luke, in part as if talking to himself and in part as if listening to a ghost, learns what he must do if he is to see his lost love again: he must go to the "western gate." The gate is, of course, a symbol, manifestly of death—perhaps by suicide—for it opens to dayfall, to night, to the end of life. To western glooms gathering, Robinson adds another symbol not unusual in his poetry: "The Dark." In this case, the double meaning is obvious: the "dark will end the dark"—death will end the living death that Luke experiences.

To emphasize his meaning, Robinson then says that the loved one has come "out of the grave" to tell him the "one way to where she is." In keeping with the symbol of the "western gate," Robinson made the season the dying time of the year—the fall. The vines and leaves have the crimson touch of the end of their life's cycle, always suggesting Robinson's awareness of nature's moods. The winds are tearing the leaves away: "The leaves will whisper there of her, and some, / Like flying words, will strike you as they fall. . . . / God slays Himself with every leaf that flies. . . ."

It was unusual for Robinson to confess to being abstruse. When readers approached him, asking him to interpret what to them was difficult to decipher in his poetry, he would shake his head sadly. On one such occasion, he told a group of ladies that they could understand his meaning if only they would read one word after another. But "Luke Havergal" poses some problems; for, as Samuel Yorks has remarked, "the voice of the poem speaks variously with the anguished lover, the loved one, a ghost, even the poet. . . ."[8] Seemingly, indeed, the ambiguity in the poems rests upon a shift in viewpoint, and for that reason the reader is left with what Mr. Yorks calls a "blurred focus." It is not that a poet has no right to shift voices but that a reader should be able to discover just how he has made the shift. Here may very well be one cause of whatever we find abstruse in this powerfully moving lyric.

No such difficulty is presented in a fourth poem concerned with the "lost love" theme: "Another Dark Lady." Whether the poem is a part of the myth and is a portrait of his "Woodland Girl," about whom Mr. Chard Powers Smith speaks at length, is not important here.[9] Clearly in this poem the suitor rejects the woman (whether or not the woman has turned the man down); for, though he apparently loved her once, he discovers in time that she is another Lilith, that her feet, far from being smooth like the beeches through which the two lovers walk together, are cloven.

"Eros Turannos," concerned with the conflict in the marriage relationship, is unquestionably one of the best of Robinson's short lyrics. Perhaps some overtones of the Emma-Herman complex may be heard, but they seem to be indistinct. Herman does not seem to fit the Judas image, nor does Emma seem ever actually to have feared him—or, if so, the indications are extremely nebulous. Robinson is far more himself, his own man, in this poem than he is in other poems usually ascribed to the myth. Indeed, "Eros Turannos" moves on a much higher level than the merely personal.

In the first place, though brief it is almost classical in its presentation of tragedy: A woman finds her husband to be a Judas, fears him, wonders why fate had ever made her choose him. Yet her pride and the love that once existed between them force her to hold him somehow, even though she exist in a home "where passion lived and died," "a place where she can hide," and though the town and harbor "Vibrate with her seclusion": the whispering, the gossip, the unkind little laughter, the maudlin curiosity of the townspeople. The intensity of this brief drama moves the reader deeply. Robinson's skillful use of nature to reinforce the emotional impact of his poem—physical environment as emphatic backdrop to situation and character as he often employed it, even in his later long narratives—is in this poem as much aural as visual: "Drawn slowly to the foamless weirs"; "A sense of ocean and old trees"; "The pounding wave reverberates / The dirge of her illusion." The tragedy of the human

relationship described in "Eros Turannos" is closed in a chorus
of melancholy in its last powerful lines:

> Though like waves breaking it may be
> Or like a changed familiar tree,
> Or like a stairway to the sea
>   Where down the blind are driven.

These are the factors that make "Eros Turannos" one of the finest
of Robinson's short poems and surely the most poignant of his
early lyrics.

Although Robinson disclaimed any debt to Browning, we
find the dramatic form so well known to the English poet in his
"Clinging Vine." "Clinging Vine" is a kind of "My Last Duchess"
in reverse and without the violence of murder, real or implied.
In Browning's poem the Duke reviles his latest partner for her
frivolity, infidelity, and her failure to appreciate him, her
husband; but his talk is addressed to an emissary of a count. In
the Robinson poem, the wife berates her husband for his infidelity. While there seems to be no question that the husband
is guilty, we somehow are left with the impression that the wife
is a scold and has been in part responsible for her husband's
dereliction. Clearly, the wife in "The Clinging Vine" rejects her
husband: "And let no more be told," she says; "For moon and
stars and ocean / And you and I are cold." There appears to
have been no adequate reason for Chard Powers Smith to relate
this poem to Emma's separation from Herman Robinson; for, in
fact, even after they were living apart, Emma saw Herman on
more than one occasion; and no evidence so far substantiated
reveals that he was unfaithful to her. Marriage in "The Clinging
Vine" meant a "wrong knot" tied; and, as has been noted, it is
the "wrong knot" concept that contains Robinson's view of
Herman and Emma's union.

The "wrong knot" tied is even more emphatically the case in
"The Woman and the Wife." In this poem, a two-sonnet sequence
and a dramatic monologue, the wife explains that her marriage
was wrong from the beginning, although she and her husband
thought that they knew it was right. They are living a lie, she
says; or he is, at least. "Passion has turned the lock," she says:
"Pride keeps the key." But her plea is that they make an end of
a relationship that was never meant to be. Like the couple in

"The Clinging Vine," they are cold; and the wife's final ironic query confirms the death of their love: "Do you ask me to take moonlight for the sun?"

Robinson treated men and women without prejudice however; and the woman is often responsible for the failure of a marriage. So it is with Genevieve—"poor Genevieve"—in "Genevieve and Alexandra," a dramatic dialogue that falls short of Robinson's usual level of accomplishment because it dwindles and falls into inconclusiveness at its close. The wife sees only that her husband's eyes wander to another woman; her sister, Alexandra, sees what is wrong and, in a perceptive revelation of the wife's fatal weakness of jealousy, diagnoses the cause of Genevieve's despair. "Do you believe," she says, commenting upon Genevieve's plaint of living in a cage, beating iron bars—

> Because a man—a rather furry man
> Who likes a woman with a dash of Eve
> To liven her insensible perfection—
> Looks now and then the other way, that you
> Are cribbed in iron for the whole blessed length
> Of all your silly days?

"He wants his house to live in," she continues. He is not, in brief, expecting too much of his wife: no more than that she recognize him for what he is and wants to be. But, like a perverse John Gorham, Genevieve will not permit her husband to fall short of perfection; nor will she use the face and eyes and womanly beauty (the dash of Eve) to recapture her husband's love. At last this "bogey-burdened" wife turns accusingly even on her own sister—her nerves "talking" at last, until Alexandra can only say "Poor Genevieve."

VI *False Values*

Broadly extended and infinitely more complex developments of the marriage situation are to be found in blank-verse narratives such as *Roman Bartholow, Cavender's House,* and *Matthias at the Door.* Certain shadows of the myth fall across both the first and last of these poems; but, except as earlier noted, attempts to relate specifically character and situation are sometimes extremely difficult. But enough of the family story intrudes upon these fictions for us to realize that the myth was in part a basis for their thematic development; and the same may be true of other marriage poems.

Roman Bartholow, however, fuses two themes rising from the myth. The union of Roman and Gabrielle is still another "wrong knot" tied. At the same time, in a somewhat less distinct way, but still deriving from Robinson's antithesis for materialism, Roman's rejection of the false material values of his family is implicit. "My father was to me a mighty stranger—" he confesses. He has lived in his "ancestral prison" long enough to know despair and hopelessness born of a knowledge that "this old ivied house of stone / Built years ago by one whose glowering faith / In gold on earth and hope of it in heaven" stands upon infirm foundations. His father's life and his own, until recent events had altered it, were premised on false values: the ancestral pattern has led to the following of false gods.

Gabrielle, whom he marries in high hope, fails to lift him from the nadir of his despondency. Fortuitously, he is saved, healed in his soul, by Penn-Raven, a neighbor and friend, a kind of amateur psychiatrist and, as the story opens, an unwilling guest in Bartholow's house. Now that Roman has found his soul and has been "born again" (a curiously repeated sequence of conflict, catharsis, and rebirth in some of Robinson's long narratives), he believes that he can build a new house: begin a new life with Gabrielle.

For Gabrielle, however, there can be no new life. Her marriage with Roman has been a loveless one. She cannot save him from his tragic plight; and she has grown not to care for what he has offered or can offer in lieu of himself and a meaningful love. Nor, as the narrative opens, does she see a place for herself in the life that her husband now wants to build. To Penn-Raven, who has developed a passion for her during his stay in Bartholow's home, she can respond only in a physical way; he fails to involve her spirit, to inspire her trust, or to capture her entire being for himself alone. And she admits to Roman, who has found himself and, Lazarus-like, is alive again: "I shall not know men, / Though I live on till all humanity / Be dry bones at my feet, and the world frozen."

Finding herself alone at last, she tells her husband that she will build no houses with him, that he had better share his new house with another who would not "shake it down" over his head. "For now," she says, "I can see nothing / Before me, or behind me. It's all gone." Roman knows and confesses that he had been wrong ever to shut her up in his impossible house, the house of despair. "It was wrong," he says, "And sadly wrong, for me to go so far / Into that darkness and to take you with me. . . ." He, however, is going into a new region where she "cannot follow"; and she drowns herself in the river that flows beyond the house and through the trees.

With that incident and with Penn-Raven's departure the story might well have concluded. A curious tale, redolent of ghosts and of the not quite real, it is closed by Umfraville, most curious of all the characters—a "scholar" who serves as a kind of spiritual adviser to Roman—with comments upon Penn-Raven, Gabrielle, and Roman himself.[10] Umfraville, we somehow conclude, is not entirely credible. Perhaps in his late discursive recapitulation of affairs, he lends himself as a unifying device. In any case, Robinson felt comfortable in employing him to explain away some of the complexities of this psychological "novel." For all that, he remains a device, and he renders less forceful the resolution of the essential conflicts.

Robinson strayed from his purpose in *Roman Bartholow*. His dual theme, stated at the outset of the poem, becomes something different as the narrative progresses. What might have been a conflict in a triangle—and seems to be at intervals—comes finally to be the story of a man psychologically disturbed but healed; of a healer who betrays the man he has brought to sanity; and of a woman who can find no reason for living and thus commits suicide. Within the limits of the tale there is no close bond between Roman and Gabrielle, and there never has been. In this respect their marriage was a wrong knot and the theme holds, even though it lacks proper emphasis. Despite the apparent affection that Roman has for Penn-Raven, that affection is illusion. The "Raven" himself, like the bird he is named after, is parasitical.

Umfraville, always outside the narrative, an uninvolved, if sympathetic, onlooker, fails to bring the tale into clear focus. Roman's words to Umfraville, at the last, put a false stress on the thematic development: "We should have known each other better / If I had known myself." For self-knowledge, on many occasions a basic theme in Robinson, is never clearly evident as his purpose in this tale. Chiefly emphasized is the theme of the healing of a soul in distress, a rebirth of Roman's spirit. And Roman's thought that he had adored Gabrielle "and outgrown her" is not quite convincing. Theirs was a wrong knot tied, and Umfraville states the fact succinctly: "There were you two in the dark together, / And there her story ends."

Cavender's House, in contrast, is simple in structure and intensely concentrated to effect a single objective. Basically, it concerns a marriage relationship ended by murder: Cavender, in a fit of passion stirred by jealousy, throws his wife Laramie over the cliff near their house by the sea. But the failure of their marriage lay in Cavender's way of life, and Robinson's denunciation of materialism is scarcely more plainly stated in any other of his poems. For Cavender is a successful tycoon, lustful for power, willing to crush any man who stands in his way of achieving , as Laramie tells him, more of his "splendid gains and benefits." Having become accustomed to power, to possessing what he wishes, walking erectly and independently with an air of authority, he buys the beautiful Laramie for his wife. Because she asserts her own personality, objecting to his overbearing way with her, his jealousy is aroused.

The narrative opens *in medias res*, twelve years after Laramie's death, which is judged a suicide. In flashbacks the reader is informed that Cavender has meantime wandered the world, plagued and conscience-striken by his act. Now, returned late at night to the scene of the tragedy, he goes into the house that he had built, lived in, and abandoned. Cavender's house is, manifestly, his life as it was and is no longer. Laramie who, he thinks, has called him back, can be no more than a figment, no matter that she seems real enough. Their conversation can be no more than a dialogue between Cavender and himself—his conscience, his memory, or his imagination. Robinson employed a cleverly conceived variant in his dramatic presentation, the more fitting here because of the setting of the real-unreal.

Cavender seeks in this last "meeting" with Laramie to learn whether she had in fact been unfaithful to him. He is not to learn, but he does discover—or perhaps he had already discovered during his tormented years of self-examination and self-recrimination—precisely why his marriage failed: because of his emphasis upon false values. But we cannot be sure that self-knowledge will bring him peace. Peace, he admits, he is afraid of. In the end

He was alone
Now, in a darker house than any light
Might enter while he lived. Yet there was light;
There where his hope had come with him so far
To find an answer, there was light enough
To make him see that he was there again
Where men should find him, and the laws of men,
Along with older laws and purposes,
Combine to smite.

Cavender will make his retribution, whatever form it is to take.
Self-knowledge will bring him to do so.

VII   *Matthias at the Door*

To the present-day reader, *The Glory of the Nightingales*
seems contrived, if it has not always seemed so to those who have
patiently read it. Such is not the case with *Matthias at the Door*.
Aside from the Arthurian legends, this poem, along with
Amaranth, strikes one as perhaps the best of the later blank-
verse tragedies. No one can doubt that *Matthias* had its roots in
the myth, in personal history. With a knowledge of the myth,
we see Dean Robinson cast as Garth; Win Robinson as Timberlake; Herman as Matthias (possibly because for a long time he
drinks excessively); and Emma (if she can emerge as a red-
haired beauty) as Natalie. But by 1930, when Robinson composed the poem, he may have found many a figure, male and
female, flickering through his imaginative eye. If he drew from
the life, his characters in this drama were surely composites of
both the sacred and the profane. Chard Powers Smith has tried
to solve parts of the puzzle, but certain pieces remain on the
table to be put in their proper positions to fill out the picture.
To relate Robinson's characters to the myth alone would be to say
indeed that they are ghosts with whom the poet is talking in an
empty room. But these are for the most part fully fleshed people,
too humanly endowed, too passionately involved with life—and
death—to be ferried back across the river Styx. Robinson was no
Charon.

The situation and the thematic emphasis of *Matthias* the poet
derived chiefly from the myth. Like Cavender, Matthias is
affluent, a materialist; but he marries Natalie because he loves

her, or believes sincerely that he does. He loses her not by
murder but through her suicide, somewhat after the manner of
Gabrielle. On the other hand, Natalie marries him because she
likes him and because, even if unhappily, he is there and at the
moment the sole possessor of the right to marry her. For Matthias
has saved Timberlake, one of his two closest friends, from death;
and for that reason Timberlake sacrifices his own love for
Natalie and wanders into the world to make of his life a waste
and to become an alcoholic. Garth, Matthias' other friend, commits suicide almost as the story opens. It may be that fact and
the fact that Matthias later finds Natalie in Timberlake's arms
that tempt one to regard this poem as a final thrusting solution
of the Emma-Herman-Win triangle. For after this discovery and
after Natalie's confession that she had always loved Timberlake,
Matthias, angry, frustrated, confused, turns to drink. With Timberlake gone, he literally drives Natalie to her death. Beyond
that act

> For a long time
> His world, which once had been so properly
> And admirably filled with his ambitions,
> With Natalie, with his faith, and with himself,
> Was only an incredible loneliness,
> The lonelier for defeat and recognition.

But Matthias needs to find the meaning of that recognition; and
Timberlake, returning to die, his life-light almost burned out as
he returns, gives it meaning when he says to Matthias

> There is a nativity
> That waits for some of us who are not born.
> Before you build a tower that will remain
> Where it is built and will not crumble down
> To another poor ruin of self, you must be born.

What follows Timberlake's death is a figment. Matthias tortured
by his losses of wife and friends, is also tormented by the
admonition, spoken by Timberlake, that he must be born again.
The "door" down in the coulee, scarcely a hundred yards below his
house, is a symbol of death. Through it both Garth and Natalie
have passed; but Matthias cannot die until he has been born,
and in his mind he hears Garth say so at the last. Nevertheless,
it is exactly at the point of Garth's reappearance as a ghostly
adviser that *Matthias at the Door* fails as a significant narrative.

The reality of the burden of the poem is broken by the intrusion of this unreality and Matthias' recognition scene is weakened. At the same time, the structure of the tale is dissipated like the frayed ends of a cable. The tragic force of the fiction would have been greater without Garth's return.

However, the reader is moved by strong empathic responses through most of the tale. It is not the deaths of Natalie and Garth and Timberlake that move him; but rather, beginning with the crisis in the poem when Natalie tells Matthias the truth about their marriage, it is the relentlessly gradual revelation of self that Matthias faces—the inevitable, inescapable realization of a man in whose mind life had once seemed such a simple thing but who now must grapple with life's infinite complexity.

VIII   A Broad View

Although Robinson was not a well-traveled man and although he did not range broadly in his experiences with life, he had the world within his purview, even if people more than places concerned him. Nowhere does this fact manifest itself more definitely than in his portraits and, generally, in his sonnets. Among these are numbered a few of Robinson's own predilections. When Louis Untermeyer wrote him late in May or early June, 1931, asking what three or four poems he liked best (for an anthology, it must be presumed), Robinson replied that he did not know certainly which three or four, but probably, he wrote, he would first choose "Ben Jonson Entertains a Man from Stratford," for one. Beyond that, he named "Mr. Flood's Party," "Flammonde," "The Man Against the Sky," or "The Master"; and for sonnets, "Many Are Called" and "The Sheaves."[11]

If this list represents a personal preference, it also contains some of his most popular as well as some of his finest poems. But it should be extended. To the longer portraits such as "Ben Jonson," we are inclined to add "Rembrandt to Rembrandt," "John Brown," "Isaac and Archibald," "Toussaint L'Ouverture," and "The Three Taverns." To "Flammonde" and "Mr. Flood's Party," along with several shorter portraits already considered, we might add "Clavering," "Cliff Klingenhagen," "John Evereldown," "Reuben Bright," and "George Crabbe"—to make an arbitrary selection. Had Robinson written no other poems but these, he would be well remembered and highly regarded.

The longer portraits (that is, the poems of moderate length) present a broad range of subjects, all of them far removed from the myth. From the Apostle Paul in "The Three Taverns," to Shakespeare in "Ben Jonson Entertains a Man from Stratford," from the Negro hero of the revolution of 1791 in Haiti in "Toussaint L'Ouverture," and the great crusading Abolitionist in "John Brown," to the nostalgia-filled portrayal of the two beloved figures of Robinson's youth, Isaac and Archibald—these form a brilliant tapestry in Robinson's poetic design. To be sure, the historical personages invited Robinson's own interpretation; and we must expect to find something of the poet himself, somewhat of his own life and thought, in their presentation. *That* is the artist's prerogative. Yet Robinson did not abuse his privilege.

Among those poems of middle length, "Ben Jonson" unquestionably deserves the high favor it has found with Robinson's readers, for the poet rose to the challenge of his great subject. Yet the seeming effortlessness of the whole poem bespeaks the needful pains that Robinson took in order to produce the effect he wanted. It is a dramatic monologue with a simple setting in the Mermaid, famed tavern of Elizabethan London. Ben Jonson and a mutual friend of Shakespeare are drinking together, and Ben is regaling his guest by making a shrewd analysis of the great poet as a man and as a playwright; and, in doing so in some of his finest, most mature and compact blank verse lines, Robinson reveals as much of Shakespeare as may be contained in a half-dozen biographies.

We scarcely need read Jonson's *Timber* or a handful of Jonson's plays to understand why he would make so much of Shakespeare's failure to follow the rules of classical drama. Robinson carefully planted the line "I tell him he needs Greek" for Jonson to repeat and then to follow with

> I'll talk of rules and Aristotle with him,
> And if his tongue's at home he'll say to that,
> "I have your word that Aristotle knows,
> And you mine that I don't know Aristotle."
> He's all at odds with all the unities,
> And what's yet worse, it doesn't seem to matter. . . .

And Jonson's language has just enough of the Renaissance idiom to lend authority to it. "D'ye wonder that I laugh?" " 'What ho, my lord,' say I." "Talk! He was eldritch at it. . . ." "Whatso he drinks that has an antic in it. . . ." "I'd stake ye coin o' the realm. . . ."

But these are the superficies. The subtleties of the poem lie first in the tightly packed lines:

> . . . and he has dreams
> Were fair to think on once, and all found hollow.
> He knows how much of what men paint themselves
> Would blister in the light of what they are;
>
> He knows now at what height low enemies
> May reach his heart, and high friends let him fall;
>
> The roiling inward of a stilled outside,
> The churning out of all those blood-fed lines,
>
> The full brain hammered hot with too much thinking,
> The vexed heart over-worn with too much aching,—
>
> He's old enough to be
> The father of a world, and so he is.

Moreover, it is the mature Shakespeare whom Robinson captured in this portrait. In keeping with the style of Shakespeare's later plays, in which we find increasingly the weak or feminine endings, Robinson's lines reveal more feminine endings than he had ever employed in his own earlier blank verse.[12]

"Rembrandt to Rembrandt," "Toussaint L'Ouverture," and "John Brown" also presume a knowledge of history and biography. Yet the first, the self-portrait of the artist rendered as self-analysis and in blank-verse lines, catches the Holland painter asking questions that Robinson may well have been asking of himself. With masterpieces already to his credit, Rembrandt, widowed now and facing the scorn of "Injured Hollanders in Amsterdam" for painting what angered civic leaders, raises questions about himself, about his art, and indeed about the possible futility of any man's efforts to achieve. In the end he decides to whip his devils "Each to his nest in hell" and to follow his own "particular consistency" in his "peculiar folly." If he must meanwhile accept obscurity, he concludes that "Oblivion heretofore has done some running / Away from graves, and will do more of it." He will go on, confident of his artistic integrity and of his artistic skill.

As in "Toussaint L'Ouverture" and "John Brown," Robinson has revealed a good part of his attitude toward life—his own, at least, as an artist: a willingness to accept the order of the world pretty much as it is, but with an insistence upon an affirmation of the individual integrity. This attitude becomes a theme that runs through a large number of his poems and is an expression of the optimism that prevailed in him, in one form or another, to the end.

CHAPTER 5

Darkness Over Camelot

QUITE POSSIBLY Robinson had planned to write all his Arthurian tales, *Merlin, Lancelot,* and *Tristram,* as a trilogy. Following the publication of *Merlin* in 1917, he stated in a letter to his good friend Lewis M. Isaacs that he was still pegging away at the *Lancelot* and that this poem was going to be longer than the earlier poem. He added: "I should like to write a Tristram, but . . . I am not sure that I might not be on safer ground if I were to go to work on another book like the 'Man' ["The Man Against the Sky"]. . . . I have a notion that the publishers may be inclined to balk at a Tristram if not possibly at *Lancelot* but I have lived long enough to realize that there is no use in worrying about trifles like that."[1] *Lancelot,* which he dedicated to Isaacs, did not reach the public until 1920; the publishers had indeed balked. But Chard Powers Smith believes that *Lancelot* was in Robinson's mind *before* he wrote *Merlin.*[2]

While the three poems can be regarded as a trilogy—and some critics have chosen to treat them so—Robinson himself looked upon *Merlin* as a poem "written in anticipation of L and G [Lancelot and Guinevere], to complement its various incompletenesses" and he warned that "the two should be read together."[3] Early in his life the poet had made acquaintance with the *Morte d'Arthur* and his version of Lancelot is drawn almost completely from the twentieth and twenty-first book of Malory. Without question Robinson knew Matthew Arnold's *Tristram and Iseult,* Swinburne's *Tristram of Lyonesse,* and Tennyson's *Idylls* long before he made his own adaptions of the legends. He once wrote, however, that "The outlines of Tristram are taken mostly from Malory, with certain elements of the French version as followed by Swinburne."[4] In the same letter he noted that he had made some transpositions of time and place and had invented Andred's role as a murderer.

However, Robinson's concern was assuredly not with his sources but with the essentials of the three romances that lent themselves so admirably to his purposes. But whether those purposes encompassed as much of the poet's personal history—the relationship of Herman, Emma, and himself—as Mr. Smith implies, is difficult specifically to determine. Certain scenes in *Tristram* very likely reflect Robinson's experiences at Herman's cottage on Capitol Island on the Maine Coast.[5] Moreover, Emma as Vivian or Guinevere or Isolt of Ireland is also an interesting possibility for speculation that belongs rightfully to the realm of biography or autobiography and to the Robinson myth. But the legends do bear, directly or indirectly, upon Robinson's thematic treatment of love in the three romances.

I   *Three Loves*

In his study of Robinson's Arthurian tales, Frederic Carpenter, for example, analyzed Merlin's love of Vivian as sensual; Lancelot's of Guinevere as partly sensual, partly spiritual; and Tristram's of the dark Isolt as all-inclusive and undivided, a complete love. "Tristram," Mr. Carpenter writes, ". . . . describes a love which is neither a sensuous escape from thought, like Merlin's nor a conflict of loyalties, like Lancelot's. . . . Whatever the causes, the three loves of Merlin, Lancelot, and Tristram came to three different but obviously related ends. Merlin's ended in spiritual defeat; Lancelot's ended in suffering, which, however, promised the hope of salvation; Tristram's ended in spiritual victory."[6]

Ellsworth Barnard presents a somewhat different version of the theme of love in the three poems. "Through *Merlin* from the beginning," he writes, "in the rhythm of the verse, there echoes a premonition of the end of every love and every kingdom born or built in Time; and also, though heard but faintly in the distance, the faith that after every ending will come a new and a better beginning. . . ."[7] For Lancelot and Guinevere, however, "The world of romantic love and romantic royalty is passing not for a time but . . . forever." In *Tristram,* Mr. Barnard maintains, Robinson, having rejected the philter, "attempted to rationalize the lovers and their story," even though he did not quite "exorcise the fairy-tale atmosphere that pervades the legend in its earliest surviving forms—the remoteness, the brightness, the innocence of sin, the uncomprehending welcome, submission, or opposition accorded to life's irrational events."[8]

Chard Powers Smith does not consider all three legends as parts of one piece; and historically he is correct in regarding *Merlin* and *Lancelot* as two poems definitely planned and related, a "double epic."[9] He nevertheless makes distinctions about the treatment of the theme of love in these two romances. "Vivian," he says, "is idealized sensuous beauty, in love not with Merlin but with her preserved adolescent image of him as the great highbrow. . . . She is an intellectual woman seeking self-fulfillment, and a female mystic who transcends the illusion of time in the emotionally packed eternal moment."[10] Guinevere, in contrast, is "Heavenly Beauty, in love with Lancelot as he is each instant, at first blinded by passion to his mystical need but finally perceiving it and surrendering herself to it."[11] Smith maintains that Isolt's "state of grace was not of the full, impersonal glory of Guinevere's and Lancelot's, but it was complete self-loss. . . ."[12]

II *Worlds in Disorder*

We can see, in these critical approaches, rather broad variations in attitudes among Robinson's interpreters. Perhaps, for the moment, it would be useful to return to some comments that Robinson made regarding his treatment of the legends as he wrote about them in letters to his friends and acquaintances. One of the most direct of these he made to a young scholar who was interested in *Tristram*:

> In writing Tristram, I was merely telling a story,
> using the merest outline of the old legend. Perhaps
> I should say adapting rather than using. There is
> no symbolic significance in it, although there is
> a certain amount in *Merlin* and *Lancelot,* which were
> suggested by the world war—Camelot representing
> in a way the going of a world that is now pretty
> much gone. But possibly these two poems may be
> read just as well as narrative poems with no inner
> significance beyond that which is obvious. There is
> no "philosophy" in my poetry beyond an implication of

> an ordered universe and a sort of deterministic
> negation of the general futility that appears to be
> the basis of 'rational' thought.[13]

Robinson was deeply affected by World War I. He saw it as the beginning of the end for a civilization into which he had been born and in which he had already lived for forty-five years. Although the crumbling of his world which had, he thought, been built on rotten foundations is not the only thematic development in his Arthurian tales, it is a significant one that is underlined again and again, especially in *Merlin* and in *Lancelot*.

For Robinson used King Arthur and Camelot as a "mirror" for men to look into and find the causes for the destruction of their world. In fact, he repeated the words. First, as Merlin leaves Vivian at Broceliande, he says to her: "This time I go because I made him [Arthur] king, / Thereby to be a mirror for the world." And no doubt, in creating Arthur's kingdom, Merlin had in mind the image of chivalry and the chivalric code as a basis for a great civilization. Second, in perceiving that Camelot is doomed and that Merlin is aware that its foundations are cracking, Vivian says:

> You made him King
> Because you loved the world and saw in him
> From infancy a mirror for the millions.
> The world will see itself in him, and then
> The world will say its prayers and wash its face,
> And build for some new king a new foundation.

Third, the mirror symbol is used when Merlin tells Arthur's fool, Dagonet, of his original intent at Camelot:

> I came to see the King,—but why see kings?
> All this that was to be in what I saw
> Before there was an Arthur to be king,
> And so to be a mirror wherein men
> May see themselves, and pause.

But it is the death of Arthur's world, of our world in image, that is so insistently iterated in *Merlin*, like the ominous rolling beat of timpani behind strings and woodwinds or crashing climactically in the background of a full orchestra. Even at the beginning of the poem Gawaine forcasts the end. "No, I like not this day," he says. "There's a cloud coming over Camelot / Larger than any that is in the sky. . . ." And what will come, will come, not only because Arthur has carried on an incestuous relationship with his sister, thereby begetting Modred who is to overthrow him, but also because he weakly permits his Queen to take Lanceolt as a lover, dependent as he is upon Lancelot's great leadership to maintain his kingdom. These are the rotten foundations upon which Arthur's kingdom is built.

Lamorak, reviewing these unfortunate affairs with Kay, says "It's all too strange, and half the world's half crazy!" And Kay replies cynically: "I say the King is dead; / The man is living, but the King is dead. The wheel is broken." Meanwhile, Arthur discourses with Merlin about "this infected world" where he has sinned and erred; where he has built palaces on "sand and mud" and hears them crumbling. Later, Dagonet, expressing his contempt for war as the activity of irrational men, complains to Bedivere that Lancelot makes a war of love, Arthur a war of madness, and Modred a war of his ambition. With caustic irony Dagonet says "I'm glad they tell me there's another world, / For this one's a disease without a doctor." Bedivere answers him: "No, not so bad as that. . . . Another age will have another Merlin, / Another Camelot, and another King." He recognizes that the end has come for Arthur.

In the last scene of all, in *Merlin*, when Dagonet is with Merlin, there is talk between them of Arthur's "upheaving empire," of a "black and red and ruin / A wild and final rain on Camelot," and of the "darkness over Camelot." And what is said of the dead kingdom in *Merlin* rolls on in equally ominous beats in *Lancelot*. Arthur himself admits that the "King has had his world / And he shall have no peace." His Queen stolen by Lancelot, Gawaine's hate, and Modred's anger and ambition, "Will make of my Round Table, where was drawn / The circle of a world, a thing of wreck / And yesterday—a furniture forgotten." And Bors talks of the world of Arthur's name that has become a "dying glory." Lancelot tells Gawaine, "Your world, my world, and Arthur's world is dying, / As Merlin said it would," and Bors also speaks about "this played-out world of ours." But the most devastating line in *Lancelot* is one spoken by Gawaine: "The world has paid enough for Camelot." Robinson himself considered this line as the most significant one in the two poems.[14]

Only once is mention made in *Tristram* of the death of Arthur's kingdom and that comes in Gawaine's thoughts as he leaves Isolt of the White Hands in her garden. He reflects on Tristram's going to be made a knight of the Round Table that had been "So long the symbol of a world in order," and that was "Soon to be overthrown by love and fate / And loyalty forsworn." Two other worlds crumble in this poem: the world of love that Tristram and the dark Isolt have built, only to lose; and the world that might have been for Isolt of Brittany had Tristram returned to her. For Tristram is her world.

Thus we may see that whatever else he might have intended to say in *Merlin* and *Lancelot,* Robinson clearly used Arthur, Camelot, and the Round Table as symbols of his own civilization —one that also, even if for different reasons, stood on infirm and rotten foundations. In this instance he employed once again the theme of antimaterialism: a lust for power rather than for the flesh. His motivation, consciously or unconsciously directed, may have sprung from a certain aspect of the myth—a rejection of his father and his older brother Herman and the material standards by which they were governed. But it may have derived as easily from his own horror of the great war in Europe, his idealist's response to the brutality of the struggle, the senseless waste of life, and the total capitulation to unreason.

With the causes of that war, rooted as they were in grasping for economic power and a consequent expansion of empire, Robinson was obviously not directly concerned; but he quite obviously perceived it. We should not look into his poetry expecting to find a full-blown polemic on social and economic theory. For this reason we must dismiss as casual and extremely tenuous his statement to Hermann Hagedorn that "If one insist, Lancelot, in this poem [*Merlin*] and in L and G, may be taken as a rather distant symbol of Germany . . ."; but, he warned wisely, "the reader will do well not to make too much of this or to carry it too far."[15] His simpler interpretation of *Merlin,* and one that finds expression in a line or two of the poem, we can accept more readily: "I have made him [Merlin] without any legendary authority, such a lover of the world as to use Arthur and his empire as an object lesson to prove to coming generations that nothing can stand on a rotten foundation."[16] The parallels between the disintegration of Arthur's medieval civilization and what Robinson regarded as the collapse of our own are, therefore, plainly marked. The poet's own private disillusionment is projected into these legends.

III *The Torch of Woman*

In his letter to Hagedorn, Robinson noted two other aspects of *Merlin* and *Lancelot* that need further exploration: "Galahad's 'light,'" he wrote, "is simply the light of the Grail, interpreted universally as a spiritual realization of Things and their significance. I don't see how this can be made any more concrete, for it is not the same thing to any two individuals. The 'torch of women' is to be taken literally."[17] We need not cavil over Robinson's use of the term "light" nor his insistence upon a variable interpretation of it. He used it with the same force and with the same implicit meaning with which Shakespeare employed it in, say, *Othello;* and, moreover, he employed it to effect a simple contrast to another recurring symbol, "dark." "Light" as knowledge, intelligence, wisdom, perspicacity, understanding— perhaps even an intuitive comprehension of the mystical: all meanings are acceptable. The last line of his "Credo" ("I feel the coming glory of the Light") is a typical instance. We could wish that he had been more explicit about his phrase "a spiritual realization of Things and their significance." But it is Robinson's provocative expression "the torch of woman" that should be taken as symbolic: ". . . the torch / Of woman, who, together with the light / That Galahad found, is yet to light the world."

"Torch" as a symbol of enlightenment we accept readily. But it is difficult to consider such a symbol as a "literal" interpretation of the term. The expression "the torch of woman"—that is, woman as a torch—must, in its connotative force, turn in two directions: woman as an inspirer, as a producer of enlightenment, knowledge; and as a producer of that flame of love or passion that moves even the mightiest of men. The symbol is unusual in Robinson's poetry; indeed, it seems applicable only to the Arthurian tales or possibly also to Zoë in *King Jasper.* But it is fair to say that in the ten-year progress of his writing of the Arthurian tales, Robinson reached his greatest heights in the development of the character of woman: not singly in either first or last, but in the over-all portraiture as it evolved in Vivian, Guinevere, Isolt of Ireland and, unforgettably, in Isolt of the White Hands. In fact, the women in these narratives are in many respects his most maturely conceived females.

Vivian serves perfectly as a torch to set fire to Merlin's too-long restrained passion, to stir the physical man, not the sage and prophet. Robinson's language, as seductive as his ardent temptress, is filled with fire images. The lines "The lady Vivian in a fragile sheath / Of crimson, dimmed and veiled ineffably / By the flame-shaken gloom . . ." introduce the night of love that these two are to experience in Broceliande in Brittany. For her part, Vivian knows that her blood tingles in wonderment as Merlin approaches her. His "unseen advance among the shadows / To the small haven of uncertain light / That held her in it as a torch-lit shoal / Might hold a smooth red fish . . ." affects her so that even her skin *listens*. She is a "swimming crimson / Between two glimmering arms." She is a "flower of change and peril," the "wayward fragrance of a rose / Made woman by delirious alchemy." She kisses with "hot lips that left / The world with only one philosophy / For Merlin or for Anaxagoras. . . ." Hers is a "dusky loveliness' there in the candlelight; and when she smiles at him, her eyes "that made a fuel of the night / Surrounding her, shot glory over gold / At Merlin, while their cups touched and his trembled."

Robinson's Vivian is not the medieval enchantress but "The beauty of all ages that are vanished / Reborn to be the wonder of one woman." And she is Robinson's creation. It matters not at all that she may have been a figment drawn from the life that the poet had dreamed of having with a woman he loved, with a love never meant to be. Here in miniature is the sensuous creature, the torch of passion. As such a woman, she is closer to Isolt of Ireland than she ever is to Guinevere, though both Guinevere and the Irish Isolt are women made for love.

But Guinevere, even as we first meet her in *Lancelot*, knows that the torch she had at one time been for her knight burns less intensely now. For in the faint shadows cast by the flickering flame she sees the inevitable death of their passion. During moments of reflection her eyes tell "no more their story of old happiness." She can say to her lover, "I saw your face, and there were no more kings"; but she speaks in the past tense. Then he knows the trick of her eyes "As he knew the great love that fostered it, / And the wild passionate fate that hid itself / In all the perilous calm of white and gold / That was her face and hair. . . ." Because he loves her, he snatches her from the trial by fire at the very moment the faggots are lit. But their escape to Joyous Guard is not a honeymoon, interrupted as it is by Arthur's army and a war sustained by Gawaine's hate.

At Joyous Guard, Guinevere's torch flickers and goes out: not because her love for Lancelot has died, but because she knows that they can never find permanence in their love. Too much stands in their way: not Arthur only, as her husband. No matter how hot her fire and Lancelot's had burned, it was not enough to last. For Lancelot must now seek *his* "Light," not the light that she had for a time become for him. She can be a penitent in a nunnery.

Despite Guinevere's great beauty, despite our ready sympathy for a woman who has been forced into a mismatch at her father's command, we cannot quite forget Dagonet's words about her in *Merlin*: that she is a "woman with corn-colored hair" who has "pranked a man with horns." It is difficult to imagine how such a woman could become for Robinson a symbol of "Heavenly Beauty," beautiful as Guinevere is. Rather, she is a mature woman, quite knowing of the uses of the world, made aware ultimately of her helplessness in the face of passion and what she believes to be—and what is—the one great love of her life. She despairs over the gradual deterioration of that love and turns finally to do penance for her sins. For if Arthur's kingdom is a thing built on mud and sand, falling now from the weight of its own corruption, she has abetted and hastened its fall through her adulterous relationship with Lancelot. Therefore Lancelot must seek his "Light" and not try to recapture a world that for her and for him is lost. She will choose seclusion, meditation, prayer, her golden hair shorn and the fire in her blue eyes paled.

Each of these two legends, *Merlin* and *Lancelot*, has its own structural integrity, but their ties are close. Each is alive with a woman of great power and intensity of spirit. Yet, undeniably, while both Vivian and Guinevere are torches lit to inspire a man's passion, the latter is by far the more complex and maturely conceived woman. Vivian is merely an enchanting female. Guinevere recognizes the tragic circumstances into which she is cast and thereby grows and becomes the more enduring. Her human error—and Lancelot's—has often changed the course of history; indeed, by her own confession, it "brought on the end / Of Arthur's empire." Vivian reaches no such heights of passion and anguish and terrifying despair to which Guinevere lifts herself when she pleads with her lover not to force her back to Camelot but to take her to France. Vivian cannot stir Merlin as Guinevere stirs Lancelot over the change he has wrought in his beloved. Vivian displays no such depth of character as Guinevere reveals when, with Lancelot seeking her out at the nunnery, she can say with wisdom, "There is nothing now / That I can see between you and the Light / That I have dimmed so long."

However restrained Robinson may have been by the limitations of his sources, these women are his own creation just as, indeed, are his renderings of the tales as a whole. With the slender thread of their fragile beauty, Vivian and Guinevere bind the two legends together; and they may be read together. More important, however, is the fact that Guinevere, while initially a torch igniting the fire of love in Lancelot, grows in wisdom—a wisdom that transcends her lover's warrior simplicity, his lack of perceptiveness—and at the last it is her wisdom that brings him to the full realization of the world he is losing. In his darkness comes the Light.

In one respect, Guinevere turns back to Vivian, the symbol of sensuous beauty and the torch of passion; in another, she turns forward to Isolt of Ireland who is all love. But Isolt of the White Hands, who knows that "wisdom was never learned at any knees, / Not even a father's and that father a king" and whose child's mind clasps and treasures a love she only dreams of possessing, comprehends painfully the tragedy that has destroyed both Tristram and the Irish Isolt and that has all but vanquished her. The wisdom that she has acquired, however, is not one she can share with anyone, as she lives by the Brittany sea with the white birds flying.

Just how or when the "torch of woman," along with Galahad's "Light," is to illuminate the world, Robinson does not make clear. We are inclined rather to return to the significant theme of a world lost—whatever world it is: a kingdom, a civilization, or a world of love—or a world damned. We may conclude that the legends bespeak a "reconciliation of human hopes and purposes" that "apparently count for nothing," as one critic contends.[18] We may weigh the alternative that Bedivere suggests:

> We pass, but many are to follow us,
> And what they build may stay; though I believe
> Another age will have another Merlin,
> Another Camelot, and another King.

Tristram is, in any event, linked to its predecessors in Robinson's use of the Arthurian material, less by the "lost world" theme than by the thematic pattern of the woman sought and lost, a theme that may have involved the Robinson myth. Chard Powers Smith has said all that can be said now, if not for all time, about that aspect of the tales. Robinson was never more involved with his subjects in the longer poems (save perhaps for "Captain Craig" and *The Man Who Died Twice*) than in *Merlin, Lancelot,* and *Tristram*. But for the sure knowledge that he was always, finally, the master of his characters, the deft framer of his plots, one might think that these stories had run away with him.

IV   A *Matter of Structure*

Some critics have belabored Robinson for lapses in the unity of *Merlin* and *Tristram,* while insisting upon the superiority of *Lancelot* both as to structure and as to the firmness and contemporaneousness of characterization. A few, for example, believe that Merlin's idyll at Broceliande is simply inexplicable; but they have, apparently, forgotten the careful motivation for Merlin's defection from Arthur's court. For Merlin had made his forecast of the shape of things to come and was bored with the court; but a more important and far more human response was that he had all too humanly become disillusioned with the very kingdom that he had created and with the king on whose head he had placed a crown. Conscience-stricken, he returned to Camelot, abandoning his enchanting Vivian and admitting that he was "old." He would never return to her, and he returned to Camelot too late to save the "world" of his own creation. It is not hard to follow the logic of such a sequence.

As for Tristram's enforced stay with Morgan—an interlude that some critics have thought destructive to the unity of the poem—one should recall that Tristram has drawn his sword against his king and is exiled. The madness that follows, born of grief and an insane anger is, after all, a part of the medieval pattern that Robinson adapted for his own uses. The hero, a great lover, the master swineherd, the minstrel—Tristram—gave little satisfaction to his hostess, whose captive knight he had unhappily become. It is best to remember that "She had made other men / Dream themselves dead for her, but not this man. . . ." And when at length he tears himself away from her, he leaves her "With anger in her eyes and injuries / Of his indifference envenoming / The venom in her passion and her pride. . . ." It is best to remember also, as was noted earlier in this chapter, that Robinson utilized Malory, with some transpositions in time and place and with a few variations made by Swinburne. To complain against Robinson's structural deficiencies is thus to pass judgment upon his attempt to render into modern format a pattern that is essentially traditional, even in Wagner. Such criticism is merely gratuitous.

The position taken by Louis Coxe regarding Robinson's "overelaboration of the obvious and [his] whimsical garrulity" is sounder as critical evaluation. But this evaluation applies far less to *Merlin* than it does to *Lancelot*. Within the framework of the romantic tradition, however, Robinson's *Tristram* is not so "sticky" as Professor Coxe would have it. And to say that his characters are "more reminiscent of routine historical novels than of men and women out of myth and legend" is to ignore the poet's planned dismissal of the mystical aspects of the medieval tale, such as the philter, and his carefully devised analysis of character, however Jamesian it may have been.[19] Robinson's are unquestionably the best poetic renderings of the medieval legends in modern times. The poet adapts the tales to contemporary men and women with unusual success; indeed, he portrays them far more convincingly than those figures with whom he peoples his other blank-verse narratives.

But even if his characters fail to move some readers in an age toughened by portraits of oversexed females and frustrated anti-heroes, the sentient will remain responsive to the lyrical beauty of passage after passage in *Merlin* and *Tristram,* and to the powerful statement of tragedy in both the *Lancelot* and the *Tristram.* These three poems, taken together, are the most skillfully managed and reveal the most thoroughly disciplined poetic accomplishment in nearly all of Robinson's long fictions.

V *Tristram*

Tristram, for example, serves well to illustrate and support such general statements. Structurally it is soundly designed: its opening scene, or prologue, in Brittany, where Isolt of the white hands awaits Tristram's return, ingeniously foreshadows its closing scene, once again in Brittany, where again the white Isolt awaits Tristram, knowing at last that he will never return. The haunting repetition of the backdrop in both scenes intensifies the tragic aspect of the whole narrative. Isolt gazes always northward across the sea; her father, Breton King Howel, at the beginning desperately seeks to dissuade her from her remembrance of promises made by Tristram and at the ending tries to find words to comfort her over her loss; and the sky, in both opening and closing, is filled with "white birds / Flying, and always flying, and still flying. . . ." Moreover, these two scenes enclose and, in a sense, contain the entire dramatic spectacle—dramatic, because Robinson conceived the tragedy as a series of scenes, carefully arranging his stage in each instance to accommodate whatever characters were to appear.

In most cases, as is true in many of his long narrative poems, Robinson set his stage for a dialogue: Tristram and Isolt of Ireland; Tristram and Gouvernail; Tristram and Morgan; or Gawaine and Isolt of the white hands. Only occasionally did he place more than two characters before his audience; but when he did, he managed to describe the action so that the reader could visualize all the movement demanded of the characters. One such passage follows King Mark's celebration of his wedding to the Irish Isolt; for there, on the parapet below the feast hall in Tintagel, Tristram stands, full of bitterness and self-recrimination, joined first by Brangwaine, then by Isolt of Ireland and, after Andred has spied the lovers, by Gouvernail and Mark. Brangwaine cries out her warning to Tristram and Isolt, the lovers part from their passionate embrace, and Tristram hurls Andred violently against the wall of the parapet. When Mark appears, Andred snarls his accusation of the Queen's infidelity, asking the King to applaud his revelation. Throughout this scene, the climactic moment arriving as Tristram draws his sword against King Mark, Robinson deftly moved his characters, not permitting his reader to forget any part of the action or its sequence. Talk there is, to be sure—angry talk at times—but Robinson at no point in this significant passage fails to carry his reader swiftly along to the moment when Mark banishes Tristram from Cornwall.

In the total narrative, as has been noted, Robinson utilized the general outlines of the romance as he found them in Malory, with some variations that he drew from Swinburne. But, following the prologue in Brittany, he plunged into the midst of the basic story, the wedding feast. Thereafter, through the subtle use of backward-flashing reminiscence on the part of his characters, the poet reveals all the vital elements of the legend that led up to the "wrong knot" tied that binds the Irish Isolt to Mark irrevocably and establishes the circumstances for the impendent tragedy. These elements, indeed all elements of the *Tristram,* are so well known as to obviate an iteration of them here. But not every reader will note Robinson's adroit transitions that secure the structural integrity of his drama.

Thus the prologue ends with King Howel standing on his Breton shore where "Nothing in the cold glimmer of a moon / Over a still, cold ocean there before him . . ." and the main action begins with the same tone carried forward in these repeated and emphatic lines: "The moon that glimmered cold on Brittany / Glimmered as cold on Cornwall. . . ." Similarly, in the last lines in Part II, Queen Morgan's words to Tristram—"An error that apology too soon / May qualify too late?"—are echoed in the beginning of Part III: "Lost in a gulf of time where time was lost, / And heedless of the light queen's light last words / That were to be remembered. . . ." And as Andred lies a "crumpled shape" on the parapet at the end of Part III, so Andred becomes the first subject introduced by Mark in the beginning of Part IV. Only in Part X, the last of all, is a transition effected within the framework of one segment of the narrative; and there the shift is from Mark, who found "silence within / Silence without, dark silence everywhere— / And peace," to Isolt of the white hands. And here, too, the lines are an echo: "And peace, that lay so heavy and dark / That night on Cornwall, lay as dark that night / On Brittany, where Isolt of the white hands / Sat watching. . . ."

Just as important as such structural unity, however artfully devised, is Robinson's character delineation. Tristram and Isolt of Ireland reach the heights of the poet's finest creations—greater than Wagner's even with his music; for Robinson made a magical music of his own for them, and for Isolt of the white hands as well. He believed, having finished his last revision of the manuscript for his publishers, that he had, once and for all time, answered those critics who called his poetry cerebral only and lacking in human warmth and passion.

But it was not with his central figures only that he achieved success. He added a new dimension to the character of King Mark. At the first, of course, Mark answers to the traditional concept of the Cornish king: Tristram's uncle, "like a man-shaped goat / Appraising with a small salacious eye," who would crush the bloom of Isolt's "resisting life / On his hot, watery mouth, and overcome / The protest of her suffering silk skin / With his crude senile claws." Robinson suggests, however, that Mark's "two red and rheumy eyes" were "Pouched in a face that nature had made comely," and that only in "appearance was indulgently / Ordained to wait on lust and wine and riot. . . ." But in the end King Mark learns that in his "poor dominion" that he had of Isolt's "frail body" there was "not revenge enough / To keep even hate alive, or to feed fury"; that "There was a needlessness about it now / That fury had not foreseen. . . ." And realizing this much, he allows Tristram to return to Tintagel to see his Irish Isolt for what becomes, because of Andred's murderous knife, the last moment of the lovers' lives. Mark understands, too late, what he should have known all along; and after the lovers lie dead before him, he says to Andred, who is madly gleeful over his killings: "I am not sure that you have not done well. / God knows what you have done. I do not know. / There was no more for them—and this is peace."

Thus Mark of Cornwall has grown in self-knowledge; and now has come a moment of recognition, a quiet comprehension, an understanding of the futility of his hatred for Tristram, on the one hand, and his willful attempt to destroy a love that was indestructible, on the other. However intrusive a notation in the Robinson myth may appear at this juncture, the reader cannot but recall that Edwin's brother, Herman, too, had once a comely face which, in the excesses of his drinking, became pouched with "wine and riot," his once clear eyes red and rheumy. In the portraiture of Mark and Tintagel, Robinson's remembering mind unquestionably called up the past as he wrote his *Tristram*.

However, even the minor characters the poet carefully developed. Gouvernail becomes a kind of Horatio-Yorick figure, the trusted servant, tutor, and companion, full of deep affection for his young prince. Hearing Tristram ask him to excuse his absence at the wedding feast and hearing Tristram say "Gouvernail, you are cold," Gouvernail sighs and answers, "Yes, I am cold. . . . Here at my heart / I feel a blasting chill. Will you not come / With me to see the King and Queen together? / Or must I mumble as I may to them, / Alone, this weary jest of your complaint?" Tristram put "His hands on Gouvernail's enduring shoulders / Which many a time had carried him for sport / In a far vanished childhood. . . ." And it is Gouvernail who, with King Mark, stands watch over the bodies of the dead lovers; it is Gouvernail who, following Tristram's last request, carries the tragic tale to King Howel and to Isolt of the white hands in Brittany.

Brangwaine as Isolt of Ireland's loyal servant and companion is less clearly defined than other of the minor figures. Andred as a murderer Robinson claimed as his own invention, and so the fellow is: venomous, insanely jealous, himself in love with the Irish Isolt, a sneak, a snidely mean creature. The poet made him a consummate villain and thereby drained off the villainy from Mark in a most unusual and artfully contrived variant of the legend.

Nevertheless, the lyrical power of the poetry in *Tristram*, not greater perhaps than some of that in *Merlin*, is what Robinson strove chiefly to achieve. His unashamed use of resplendent language, his purposed avoidance of the abstract and the elliptical, and his willing embrace of purely emotional expression as opposed to the purely cerebral are never more apparent. So "Isolt of Ireland. . . . / Came nearer still to him [Tristram] and still said nothing, / Till terror born of passion became passion / Reborn of terror while his lips and hers / Put speech out like a flame put out by fire." And "When she could look at him / Again, her tears, unwilling still to flow, / Made of her eyes two shining lakes of pain / With moonlight living in them. . . ." Even Mark, filled at last with an overwhelming sadness, can speak in lines of poetic beauty: "I shall know day from night / Until I die, but there are darknesses / That I am never to know, by day or night. . . . / There are mistakes too monstrous for remorse / To fondle or to dally with, and failures / That only fate's worst fumbling in the dark / Could have arranged so well."

And Gawaine, delightful sycophant that he proves to be, woos Isolt of the white hands with an impassioned appraisal of her beauty:

"I have been seeing you for some hours," he said,
"And I appraise you as all wonderful.
The longer I observe and scrutinize you,
The less do I become a king of words
To bring them into action. They retreat
And hide themselves, leaving me as I may
To make the best of a disordered remnant,
Unworthy of allegiance to your face
And all the rest of you. You are supreme
In a deceit that says fragility
Where there is nothing fragile. You have eyes
That almost weep for grief, seeing from heaven
How trivial and how tragic a small place
This earth is, and so make a sort of heaven
Where they are seen. Your hair, if shorn and woven,
The which may God forbid, would then become
A nameless cloth of gold whiter than gold,
Imprisoning light captured from paradise.
Your small ears are two necessary leaves
Of living alabaster never of earth,
Whereof the flower that is your face is made,
And is a paradisal triumph also—
Along with your gray eyes and your gold hair
That is not gold. Only God knows, who made it,
What color it is exactly. I don't know.
The rest of you I dare not estimate,
Saving your hands and feet, which authorize
A period of some leisure for the Lord
On high for their ineffable execution.
Your low voice tells how bells of singing gold
Would sound through twilight over silent water.
Yourself is a celestial emanation
Compounded of a whiteness and a warmth
Not yet so near to heaven, or far from it,
As not to leave men wiser for their dreams
And distances is apprehending you.
Your signal imperfection, probably,
Is in your peril of having everything,
And thereby overwhelming with perfection
A man who sees so much of it at once,
And says no more of it than I am saying."

Tristram abounds, indeed, with lines that truly sing.

Certainly it must be said that this long poem (and to some extent *Merlin* and *Lancelot*) possesses a poetic character distinctly different from the great body of Robinson's work. The subject matter manifestly demanded a different treatment; but, more than that, *Tristram*, at least, represented a challenge to the Maine poet to put into his own kind of dramatic form and with his own lyrical flow the opera that had so moved him, the great love story in which, it seems, he was almost personally involved. But all three of his Arthurian romances are woven into a fabric unlike his other poems, no matter what their implications; and, as he himself said, each may be read as a narrative poem without an attempt on the reader's part to find any greater significance than the obvious.

CHAPTER 6

Bugs and Emperors

O N JUNE 3, 1920, Robinson wrote his niece, Ruth Robinson Nivison: "I shall begin to live, if all goes well, about twenty-five years after I'm dead. And that isn't a bad time to begin."[1] He had not yet achieved the popular approval that *Tristram* gave him in 1927; but that flash of recognition, with the degree of independence it brought him, dimmed in the sudden brighter light of somewhat younger poets like Sandburg, Frost, Pound, and Eliot, and a number of minor figures who followed in their company. He had no immediate American contemporaries of a stature equal to his. The great promise shown early by William Vaughan Moody failed to develop; for Moody's early death came before he could establish a significant reputation, and he is known better in our time for his quite successful, even if somewhat anemic, drama than for his poetry.

Today Robinson's comment to his niece seems to have been prophetic. Ingored by critics all through his early productive years, he finally gained the praise of a few perceptive men, even though in some instances it was grudgingly given. Those who know Robinson realize that he devoted his entire life to poetry— save only a brief interlude when he attempted fiction and drama; that he sacrificed all else to his career; and that he held to the highest standards of composition. Today, even as for many in Robinson's lifetime, these circumstances and attitudes in his artistic life command the attention and respect of poets and artists generally. Most Americans are unaware of his long struggle; for he eschewed all public gatherings, refused to read his poetry to women's clubs and poetry societies, and insisted upon going his private way with only his most intimate friends and associates.

Although Robert Frost may have manifested early in his career a reticence similar to Robinson's, Frost was by no means laconic. By 1915 his first two volumes, *A Boy's Will* and *North of Boston,* published first in England where Frost was living for a time, were reissued in the United States and found a ready market. Frost quickly became a recognized public figure. A four-time winner of the Pulitzer Prize for Poetry, honored by at least forty colleges and universities with honorary degrees in this country and by both Oxford and Cambridge in England, he obviously enjoyed his fame as poet and prophet. His magnificent voice and his always sharp sense of the dramatic charmed his listeners, just as the essentially romantic flavor of his poetry, its tinge of the metaphysical, its wit and high-pitched irony endeared him to his readers. There are those who contend that he was Robinson's superior as a "maker." Perhaps it would be fairer to say that the two men sought different goals in their poetry. Each was superb in his own idiom and form.

Ezra Pound, however, remained almost completely the ex-patriate. He lost favor in this country and in the West generally by espousing the Fascist cause in Italy during World War II. But, although his politics and his poetry should be considered separately, he suffered the loss of his once proud position and influence in the artistic world and is now read only, if at all, by a small circle of the esoteric. When the scars are healed and his unhappy history is forgotten, perhaps his poetry will be reclaimed. T. S. Eliot continues to lose ground. His aimless repetitiveness of theme, his denial of the world he lived in, his search for comfort in the womb of the past, his negativism—all have turned early Eliot enthusiasts and followers to warmer poetic fields.

I *Prophecy Fulfilled*

Meanwhile Robinson's reputation has grown steadily. In 1946, Yvor Winters produced the first full-length critical analysis of Robinson's work. To some of the poetry he gave high praise. "Three of Robinson's later sonnets," he stated, "seem to me among the greatest of his works: 'Lost Anchors,' 'Many Are Called,' and 'The Sheaves.' In fact if one adds to these sonnets and

'The Wandering Jew' two or three of the blank verse monologues —'The Three Taverns,' 'Rembrandt to Rembrandt,' and perhaps 'John Brown,'—one probably has Robinson at his greatest."[2] As has been said by another critic, Winters did not explain *why* he thought that these poems were great.[3] But later in his study, noting that the best of Robinson's poems dealt with persons and situations, he stated that their power and significance lie in the fact that "his examination is careful and intelligent, his method is analytic, and his style is mainly very distinguished." In all, Winters concluded that Robinson had greatness; but at the same time he found a certain dryness and lack of richness in the total poetic canon.

Less reserved in his critical comment, Emery Neff in 1948 maintained that Robinson was wittier than Hardy, more mature and broader in interests than Housman, and, except for Yates, without a peer in England. "It is our fault," Neff complained, "that the world must see him as a maimed giant."[4] Ellsworth Barnard's careful analysis of much of Robinson's poetry testifies throughout to the depth and significance of the material. It is hard, Mr. Barnard wrote, "to recall any poetry of permanent significance in addition to Robinson's (except Emily Dickinson's, posthumously published and soon to be forgotten for almost a generation) that appeared during the last decade of the nineteenth century or the first decade of the twentieth."[5]

Some years ago, Louis Coxe stated that ". . . there is no American poet who has approached Robinson in the number of finished poems of high merit. . . . Of possible rivals, there is none whose claim rests on the number of finished poems nor on wholly achieved effects nor on the range and of viability of the subject."[6] In his latest study of Robinson, Professor Coxe has not qualified his earlier judgment. He recognizes the limitations in Robinson's environment and tradition and circumstances, but states that he "managed to write the finest poems written in America between 1900 and 1920." He further states: "For all the obvious repetitiousness and aridity of Robinson's later work, twenty years of productiveness, and productiveness of excellence, is an unusually long period for an American writer."[7] And Coxe concludes that Robinson is in the "front rank" of American writers. There can be little question, therefore, that Robinson is one of a handful of major poets that this country has so far produced.

II *Language and Structure*

The poetry of Robinson does not summon an impulse to parody or imitation, as has been the case with the prose of Henry James, for example, with whom Robinson is sometimes paired as an exponent of the psychological technique. Despite the often deeply involuted nature of some of Robinson's meanings, his language is simple.[8] Moreover, his style is usually unadorned by those purpling passages that some poets attempt to effect. Most of his short poems are clearly individualized, vital. Whatever may be said of his long narratives, no one complains of eccentricity in word usage or style, and they do not lend themselves therefore to mocking paraphrase. He is more often accused of prolixity; and in the late long narratives he was certainly prolix, sometimes to the detriment of his poetic power. In respect to language he owed little to his predecessors or even to his contemporaries in the nineteenth and early twentieth centuries, but in form and structure he was definitely a traditionalist.[9]

It was precisely with his plainness, his colloquial usage, that early critics of Robinson's poetry found fault. Steeped in Sidney Lanier and Bayard Taylor and Thomas Bailey Aldrich, they were uncomfortable with what they regarded as a language of the streets: harsh and completely "unpoetic." In the twentieth century the chief critical comment has been directed at Robinson's coldness, his aloofness, his intellectuality. More recently, complaints have been made about his tendency to repeat certain themes, some of which he admittedly overworked. But, even if he couched his language in traditional forms, he certainly broke with tradition by rejecting the romantic and conventionally poetic usage of both his predecessors and his contemporaries.

Robinson's language was essentially intellectual-cerebral.[10] He was suspicious of unrestrained or uncontrolled emotion, a fact usually apparent in his poetry. Yet it does not follow that he was incapable of feeling or that, because he was a New Englander and, even more, a Maine man, he could not understand or express the emotional responses of others. He consciously chose to examine the minds of men and women, but even this view cannot be regarded as an absolute or as universally applicable to his poetry. What emotion we discover in him, Floyd

Stovall remarked, is "an impersonal and cosmic emotion: the protest of a stable creation against the inevitable dissolution, the outcry of elemental matter at the ravages of time."[11]

The prevailing irony that runs through Robinson's poetic canon is only another facet of the cerebral; as such, it is to be understood and evaluated—not condemned. His irony runs in two different directions and assumes two different modes: The first is the kind of ironic wit that we see in "Isaac and Archibald"; the second is cosmic in design and intent much as we find it in *Cavender's House* and in *The Glory of the Nightingales*. Whichever Robinson utilized, however, the tone is usually impersonal; the effect is more pronounced for that reason.

Perhaps it is not entirely futile to speculate on how Robinson achieved that effect. It matters not whether he was always aware of his sentence structure—syntax, if we wish—as a means of eliciting certain responses. He seems usually to have been most sharply aware of structure; aware, too, of the particular impact upon the reader he could expect by arranging his words in particular relationships. Seldom did he conceive a poem in his head and dash it onto paper as rapidly as it had come to him. His irony, especially in the short poems, is sharper or more humorous, as the case may be, when he put a word in a certain position in a line. Robert Frost, as has been said, saw the power in the repetition of the word "thought" as it appears in the next to last stanza of "Miniver Cheevy."

> Miniver thought and thought and thought
> And thought about it.

The position of the fourth "thought" accounts for the weighted irony of the entire stanza. Similarly, the adjective "ripe" in the first line of the fourth stanza ("Miniver mourned the ripe renown") enhances the irony of the first two lines. We could insist that Robinson was concerned with alliteration chiefly in this instance; or we could likewise note that the word "ripe" has a peculiarly effective meaning as well. But its position in the sentence, a position of emphasis, is equally significant. Looking backward to "mourned" and forward to "renown," it becomes the key to the ironic statement.

Patently the phrase "With a slight kind of engine" in the sestet of "How Annandale Went Out" is so placed in the sentence as to stress the irony of the whole poem. Likewise the position of both "slight" and "engine" in the syntactical arrangement may effect the reader's response. Another arrangement ("with an engine that was slight") might distort both the metrical pattern and the natural rhythm of the phrase and thus bring about an entirely different response from the reader. Although no full study of Robinson's poetic syntax has yet appeared, examples of the kind illustrated are numerous in the poet's work.[12]

That Robinson was conscious of the problems is confirmed in his comment to Sophia Peabody to the effect that often the word best suited to the meaning of a line fails to serve the metrical pattern.[13] It was for that reason, in fact, that he worked so long and so painfully at times to select a word that fitted all his purposes. Close examination of his poems shows that his youthful preoccupation with words and with word play remained always with him. As he developed his power of expression, he became sensitively attuned to word values and to the relationships of words within the framework of any poetic structure, whether a phrase or a sentence.

Yet despite his concern for words, Robinson made language and structure subserve his chief end in writing: the creation of a poem that had content and meaning. He almost never wrote on trivial subjects; and while not all his poems are by any means equally significant or equally good as poetry, most of them contain something of human value, something that dignifies the human equation.

III *Ideas and Attitudes*

That Robinson did not develop a well-ordered body of philosophy is now a commonplace among his critics. To Yvor Winters he "was not a systematic thinker, and his thought shows conflicting tendencies."[14] Winters calls Robinson a "counter-romantic" and can find only an "indistinctly perceptible" change in the poet's thinking from the beginning of his career to the end. Ellsworth Barnard asserts that Robinson "is correct in denying that he is a systematic thinker, and it was honesty as well as modesty that led him during his life to discourage attempts to extract from his writings a complete and coherent philosophy."[15] Even the latest of Robinson's critics and biographer, Chard Powers Smith, states that "If philosophy is the attempt to arrive at reality by some logical system, Robinson had no philosophy and wanted none."[16]

Still, Robinson was not destitute of ideas. He held to certain beliefs and to certain concepts about man as a microcosm and the universe as his macrocosm. The student of the Maine man has two courses open to him in his search for Robinson's essential ideas and attitudes, and one is incomplete without the other: The first is to pursue them as they are revealed in his poetry; the other is to examine and extract his private statements and utterances as they appear in his letters. Both are, after all, records of the man's mind.

Yet Robinson's critics are strangely at odds over the interpretation of his views. Seemingly, the difference rises because those who have worked over the poetry may be reading into it a much more highly involved and complex pattern of thinking (along with a careful explication of its environmental and psychological or even its mystical derivations) than Robinson's usually straight-forward statements warrant; and many of these critical evaluations have been made without attention to the letters. There are those who contend that poetry should speak for itself, that it needs no biographical or autobiographical undergirding. That contention is sound enough so long as the critic is concerned with what a poem says and means—in its simple form. But too often this critic speaks for the poem and, what is worse, insists upon analyzing the poet's life and mind in terms of only the poetry. Such a procedure often leads the critic to draw quite debatable conclusions.

The differences also rise because Robinson's total production over more than forty years of writing is one of the largest collections in American literature. The differences rise, moreover, because even those letters so far gathered—and they are not all available by any means—present a formidable, perhaps an insurmountable, challenge to the scholar. Yet even those scholars who have examined all the poetry and many, if not all, of the available letters disagree with one another.

Surely Robinson cannot have been each or all the men he is portrayed as being: romantic, counter-romantic, Calvinist, Transcendentalist, pessimist, cynic, mystic, determinist, exponent of the free will. Probably the truth is that he may have been many of these men at different moments in his life; or, at any rate, he may have utilized one viewpoint in one poem, another viewpoint in another poem. How otherwise do we reconcile the widely divergent attitudes expressed in, say, "The Octaves"—

> . . . but the wake
> That melts and ebbs between that friend and me
> Love's earnest is of life's all-purposeful
> And all-triumphant sailing, when the ships
> Of Wisdom loose their fretful chains and swing
> Forever from the crumbled wharves of Time

with Robinson-Shakespeare when he says

> It's all Nothing.
> It's all a world where bugs and emperors
> Go singularly back to the same dust,
> Each in his time; and the old, ordered stars
> That sang together, Ben, will sing the same
> Old stave tomorrow.

These are variants contradictory enough to make us wonder, especially as in the same volume in which the latter lines appear we read the following from "The Man Against the Sky.":

> If there be nothing after Now,
> And we be nothing anyhow,
> And we know that,—why live?

Doubtless a good deal of "Ben Jonson Entertains a Man from Stratford" is as much Robinson as it is Shakespeare—as much, say, as Robinson is Paul in "The Three Taverns." "The Man Against the Sky" is sometimes regarded as Robinson's most nearly complete statement of whatever philosophy of life he held; and that statement is an unequivocal affirmation of life and a denial of eternal death. In no other poem, however, do we find a similar firmness of attitude. The doubts and fears raised and overcome in "The Man" appear and reappear in later poems unresolved.

The reader of Robinson's poetry should begin his study with an examination of the themes that are predominant in it, that are repeated and emphasized, and that are sometimes identified with statements that he made in his letters. One of these, as noted earlier, is the poet's antithesis toward materialism. The theme, so often appearing in his poems, both short and long, precisely expresses a viewpoint that Robinson held throughout his life. It is more insistently expressed in his early poetry, for in the later work his attacks diminish in intensity.

A second theme that runs through a large body of his work, and one for which parallels may be found in his letters, contains a concept that Robinson closely adhered to in his own thought and conduct: namely, that in self-knowledge and possibly only in self-knowledge could one attain the proper fulfilment of life. From "*Captain Craig*" and "*Roman Bartholow*" to "*The Glory of the Nightingales*" and *Matthias at the Door*" the theme resounds. And a third is not so much theme as observation or comment: an apparent failure in life may be redeemed by some quality of character, some degree of individual integrity. And, finally and fourth, is the view that society, a civilization, built on the shifting sands of corruption falls by the weight of its corruption. One sees it emerge in the Arthurian tales as well as in "*King Jasper*."

It is significant to note that in the last of Robinson's poems, *King Jasper*, some hope is expressed. Not all is a negation even if Jasper's kingdom falls. For Zoë—call her knowledge, love, truth, or all three—is alive and will go on. Indeed, Mr. Barnard takes what is an irrefutable position when he says that "Robinson's attitude toward life is essentially affirmative."[17] Yet Robinson's views about life do change although some of his idealism prevails even to the end. That idealism progresses from his almost absolute position as a young man, as it may be seen in the early poems as well as in his letters to both Harry Smith and Arthur Gledhill, to what he called a "desperate optimism," and finally to a kind of quiet acceptance of the world and all the people in it very much as they are.

"There is no sense in saying that this world is not a pretty difficult place, but that isn't pessimism," he wrote to one young scholar in 1931. "The real pessimist sees too much of one thing, and the optimist is too likely to see only what he wishes to see— or perhaps not to see at all beyond the end of his famous nose."[18] Such light banter scarcely covers a broken heart or a serious disillusionment; it says exactly what Robinson intended to say and is neither denial of life nor an escape from it but a simple recognition of the plain truth as he judged the truth to be. We may say, therefore, that if Zoë in *King Jasper* represents his final word, his last statement reveals a clinging to a hope, however tenuous and uncertain that hope might be for the reader.

Much the same thing may be said of Robinson's attitude toward religion. His early faith in God and in immortality most

clearly underwent momentous change as the years passed. The
certainties expressed in "The Man Against the Sky," "The
Octaves," "Two Sonnets," and other poems of his young man-
hood lose their firm conviction in the later poems until, in
King Jasper, we listen to Zoë saying to the King:

> If I were you, I should give Hebron's ghost
> My crown of glory, and leave the rest to God.
> I don't say what God is, but it's a name
> That somehow answers us when we are driven
> To feel and think how little what we have to do
> With what we are.

The more definite of his early views he stated in letters to
Smith through the 1890's. Toward the end of his life he wrote
meaningfully on the subject to Laura Richards, and one finds in
these letters a considerably altered attitude. On January 20,
1933, he wrote to her:

> Leaving out the Romans and the Methodists, there
> doesn't seem to be much left of the churches but
> the buildings. Even the Romans will have to
> contrive some sort of symbolic compromise before
> long; and as for the Methodists, who come nearer
> to ruling us than we suspect, they are perhaps more
> an incorporated and shrewdly organized ignorance
> than they are a church, and the Church of England
> is more like a social club, with music and trim-
> mings, than like anything in the Scriptures. The
> Christian theology has so thoroughly crumbled that
> I do not think of any non-Roman acquaintance to
> whom it means anything—and I doubt if you do. The
> Christian ethics might have done some good if they
> had ever been tried, or understood, but I'm afraid
> it's too late now. There's a non-theological religion
> on the way, probably to be revealed by science
> when science comes definitely to the jumping off
> place. It is really there now, but isn't quite
> ready to say so.

On February 13 of the same year, continuing his discussion of
the matter, he commented: "As for religion in the future, I didn't
say that it wouldn't be mystical. Of course it must be that in
order to be a religion, but it will be free from all theological

machinery. I suppose you know about the recusant gentleman who said that he might believe in the Trinity when he saw one man riding in three carriages."

On May 4, 1934, Robinson again wrote to Mrs. Richards about religion as he regarded it:

> Christianity never meant anything to me except for
> its ethics, which are often unfortunately expressed
> for the common mind. And they were evidently not
> expressed for the people but for initiates and
> specialists. What more could the man in the street,
> or the women in the house, have made of the Gospels
> and Epistles than are made of them now? But it
> would be interesting to know just what
> happened and how it all came about. Many books have
> been written about it, but they only tell us what
> the authors don't know. Literal interpretations,
> or misinterpretations, have made several hells on
> earth, and a fairly rational interpretation merely
> tells us to be good and kind—which we proceed
> immediately not to be. I don't mean you.

Whatever orthodox views Robinson may have held in the 1890's, when he wrote so unrestrainedly to Smith and Gledhill, it is perfectly clear that by 1933-34 he no longer had any faith in institutionalized religion. Indeed, if he had any religious faith at all it was personal and extremely nebulous. To attempt to define it on the basis of what he said in his poetry is a futile, even if an interesting, exercise. Even his concept of immortality was not conventional; the next world was not another world like this one, not another world with all the people going about their business as they had in this world. For our world, as he saw it (though we must make the most of what we have), is a poor place to live in.

Two enigmatic passages in *King Jasper* may reflect his latest views about immortality. Zoë tells the prince:

> "My father—my wise father, not the king—
> Told me I must, and saw for me the means
> To live when he was gone. 'For you must live,'
> He said to me, 'and sometimes wonder why;
> And you must always go your way alone.'
> And those words follow me. If we have found
> Ourselves, and in each other, why should nature

> Sunder us—just for that? I'm like a child
> Trying to find the answer, and all the while
> I know it, and am afraid because I know it.
> With you, because I love you, I'm a waif
> Afraid of nature, and of going so far
> Alone—if I must go."

Not long afterward, speaking of a spot that she and the prince have found above the king's house, she says,

> "I was up there
> This afternoon alone and found the rock—
> Just a flat rock that lay there, for no reason;
> 'What's under it?' I could not lift the rock;
> And what was under it I cannot tell you.
> And like as not there was not anything. . . ."

If Robinson intended his symbols to mean what they appear to mean, the immortality that Zoë will experience is one which she fears to face alone; and what it might be like, if there is to be one, she cannot say. The individual must face the dark beyond the dark alone, perhaps without even his Good Deeds as a traveling companion.

IV *Failing Years*

The poems discussed are not by any means all of the best of Robinson's work. But they suffice to reveal his basic themes and are representative of the finest of his poetic production. Yet more needs to be said of the last of his long narrative fictions, even though a few of them have been considered and their weaknesses and strengths pointed out. While Louis Coxe has insisted upon Robinson's stature as a poet of our times, he has also complained that "Everything Robinson wrote in blank verse in the last fifteen to twenty years of his life is too long, too diffuse, too manneristic." And, he adds, "One feels that, like James, Robinson began to enjoy his own work too much, the sound of his own voice tended to intoxicate him."[19] Mr. Coxe had no space in his brief pamphlet to defend his position, but it should be said that the last twenty years of Robinson's life span all that he wrote from 1916 until his death. The judgment is too harsh. We can accept it for perhaps a half dozen of the long narratives, but we surely must exclude *The Man Who Died*

Twice, Amaranth, and the Arthurian tales from Mr. Coxe's sweeping critical evaluation.

Robinson letters do reveal the fact that in the last four or five years of his life the poet was astounded over the way his long poems sold. He was encouraged enough, even during the early years of the depression of the 1930's, to continue to bring forth a long poem each year. But his letters also reveal the fact that, through the production of *Tristram,* he firmly believed in what he was doing—believed that he had created something substantial. After 1930, especially, he was not enamored of his own voice but simply tired and not at all well. He drove himself; and the strain, the effort, and the exhaustion show in his poetry. He lost his power of compression and precision; he lost much of his control of structure. That he produced anything at all after 1930 testifies to the strength of the man's spirit when his body had failed him. But what he produced was, admittedly, not of the quality of his earlier work.

V *A Final Judgment*

The Maine man's total dedication to poetry at a moment in American literary history when (if ever it is otherwise) a poet could not sustain life by his writing forced upon him an insular kind of existence. But this insularity was chiefly economic and geographical. Looking outward from his small corner, with those dark, penetrating merry eyes, a long slender finger pressed against his high brow, Robinson saw that what was near at hand was all the world in miniature. He himself presents no paradox; his tastes and his habits were simple. The several thousand brief letters and notes that he wrote to friends and acquaintances reveal a great concern for the mundane and the commonplace.

He warned·scholars against making a perplexity of his work when he had no intention of confusing anyone. The disposition to over-complicate what the poet designed to be simple should be discouraged. The excitement a critic engenders in this or that aspect of Robinson's poetry, wafting himself thereby to a hasty conclusion, beclouds rather than clarifies. Moreover, attempts to force a consistent pattern upon the obvious inconsistencies in Robinson are certain to be frustrated. Chard Powers Smith, for example, states that "The basic reason Robinson never passed judgment on anyone, even the comfort-anesthetized rich, even the 'victims of good luck,' was his instinctive addiction to another central Puritan tenet, that of Predestination."[20] Is it not just possible that Robinson never (or almost never) passed judgment on people because he shunned causing pain—and just possibly because he had experienced so much pain himself? Oversensitive, living his entire life with his skin turned inside out, he was restrained, with rare exceptions, even in his criticsm of the work of younger poets. More often than not he would suggest a fault in a line or a stanza and then protest that probably he was wrong. Indeed, his letters are filled with qualifications to take the sting from comments or to reduce to harmlessness what might have been regarded as peremptory.

His business was the writing of poetry. His poetry was concerned almost exclusively with people: not so much with what these people did but with what they thought and how and why. His own quiet way of living, his humility, his genuine warmth, his capacity for friendship, his large humor—all are exemplary. In some respects he came like Matthew Arnold into a world that was already dying, if not dead; and he waited, after his fashion and his fancy, for a new world to be born. But he did not like the shape of things to come and was glad, as he told Mrs. Richards, that he was on his way out of it. In this respect he did not grow with his times nor adapt himself fully to the rapid changes that were taking place.

Nor did he wish to enlist himself in the ranks of the shapers; he wished only to be a poet. He had faith in the thought that he was doing some good for some of his readers. Too honest, too much the artist of integrity, he would not fall to the level of the popular and the banal to be a propagandist or a leader of popular causes. He set his standards high; he made the most rigorous demands of himself; and after fifty years of unrewarded struggle, he at length achieved both recognition and distinction. We can find no greater tribute to man's courage, to his prevailing will to seek, like Palissy, the moment of glory in creation, than in the life of this American poet. Beneath the disarming simplicity of the exterior man and the quiet, sometimes lonely life he lived, is revealed, to those who search, a rare, an infinitely warm and gifted human being, an artist of discernment and of lofty purpose. Today, Robinson stands among a scant handful of American poets who have proved themselves capable of sustained production of poetry of the highest order.

Notes and References

Chapter One

1. To Emma Shepherd Robinson, October 23, 1931.
2. See Hermann Hagedorn, *Edwin Arlington Robinson* (New York, 1939), pp. 4-6.
3. Laura E. Richards, *E. A. R.* (Cambridge, Mass., 1939), p. 7.
4. *Breaking Into Print.* Compiled by Elmer Adler (New York, 1937), p. 163.
5. To Laura E. Richards, June 19.
6. September 27, 1890.
7. Dated Gardiner, December, 1890.
8. Peter Deckert, *Edwin Arlington Robinson: A Study in Influences* (Philadelphia, 1955), p. 6.
9. *Ibid.*, Appendix B, pp. 187-92.
10. *Ibid.*
11. *Breaking Into Print*, p. 166.
12. *Untriangulated Stars* (Cambridge, Mass., 1947), p. 143. Hereafter noted simply, *US*.
13. Deckert, *op. cit.*, pp. 125-26.
14. *Ibid.*
15. *Ibid.*, pp. 123-44, *passim.*
16. To Gledhill, February 23, 1889.
17. Harvard Collection.
18. *Ibid.*
19. *Ibid.*
20. *US*, p. 4.
21. *Ibid.*, p. 11.
22. New York: Fords, Howard, and Hulbert, 1860. Intro.
23. Harvard Collection. 1896.
24. *Breaking Into Print*, p. 165.
25. *US*, pp. 119-20.
26. *Ibid.*, p. 24.
27. *Ibid.*, p. 52.
28. Quoted in Lewis M. Isaacs, "E. A. Robinson Speaks of Music," *New England Quarterly*, XXII (1949), 499-510.
29. *US*, p. 49.
30. *Ibid.*, p. 69.
31. *Ibid.*, pp. 144-45.
32. *Ibid.*, p. 98.

Chapter Two

1. To Gledhill, October 28, 1893. Harvard Collection.
2. *Ibid.*
3. *Ibid.*
4. *Selected Letters of Edwin Arlington Robinson* (New York, 1940), p. x. Hereafter noted simply, *SL*.
5. *US*, p: 150.
6. *Ibid.*, p. 156.
7. August 20, 1895. Harvard Collection.
8. *US*, p. 265.
9. See *US*, pp. 266-78; also see Emery Neff *Edwin Arlington Robinson.* pp. 76 ff.
10. *US*, p. 268.
11. *Ibid.*, p. 271.
12. *Ibid.*, p. 272.
13. *Ibid.*, p. 275.
14. *Ibid.*
15. *Ibid.*, p. 286.
16. *Ibid.*, p. 285.
17. To Hays Gardiner, November 2, 1898.
18. Undated letter from Gardiner, Maine. Probably early summer, 1900.
19. August 27, 1899.
20. April 27, 1900.
21. *US*, p. 160.
22. January 31, 1904.
23. New York Public Library Collection.
24. May 15, 1905.
25. New York Public Library Collection.
26. To Hays Gardiner, March 9, 1913.
27. Sheldon Cheney, *The Theater* (New York, 1935), p. 500.
28. *Ibid.*, pp. 500-1.
29. March 9, 1913.
30. Colby College Collection.
31. *Ibid.*
32. *Ibid.*
33. August 18, 1927. Williams College Collection.
34. September 18, 1900. New York Public Library Collection.
35. March 18, 1916. Colby College Collection.
36. March 18, 1916.
37. February 11, 1918.

Chapter Three

1. The Brower collection, the Untermeyer collection, and the Barrett collection, for example.

2. Ellsworth Barnard, *Edwin Arlington Robinson* (New York, 1952), p. 2.
3. Quoted in Leon Edel, *Literary Biography* (Toronto, 1957), pp. 49-50.
4. *Ibid.*
5. An unpublished memoir written by a member of the family.
6. Louis Coxe, *Edwin Arlington Robinson* (Minneapolis, 1962), p. 10.
7. *US*, p. 148.
8. Letter to this writer, March 31, 1964.
9. David Nivison, "Does it Matter How Annandale Went Out?" *Colby College Quarterly,* (December, 1960), pp. 174-75.
10. *US*, p. 133.
11. See Chard Powers Smith, *Where the Light Falls* (New York, 1965), pp. 109-10.
12. See Nivison, *op. cit.*, pp. 182-83; and Coxe, *Edwin Arlington Robinson*, p. 11. Whether Robinson discussed his relationship with Emma in sessions with Dr. Merrill Moore, the poet and psychiatrist, is a matter of conjecture.
13. Malcolm Cowley, "Edwin Arlington Robinson: Defeat and Triumph," *New Republic,* CXIX (December 6, 1948), 226-30.
14. Nivison, *op. cit.*, p. 184.
15. *Ibid.*, pp. 184-85.
16. *US*, pp. 137-38.
17. See, for example, William C. Childers, "Edwin Arlington Robinson's Proper Names," *Names,* III (1955), 223-29.
18. Egbert S. Oliver, "Robinson's Dark—Hill-to-Climb Image," *Studies in American Literature* (New Delhi, 1965).
19. October 28, 1896. Harvard Collection.

Chapter Four

1. Ellsworth Barnard has gone farther and more successfully with classification than any other of Robinson's critics. Yet even he qualifies his presentation of the failure theme, for example, by admitting that "the lines of classification are not always sharp, straight, or unyielding; that sometimes the boundary between success and failure is hard to draw, and that often the balance in which happiness and misery is weighed is hard to read" (p. 144).
2. *The Man Who Died Twice* is one of the shortest of Robinson's blank verse narratives, containing only about twelve hundred lines.
3. Isaacs, *op. cit.*, p. 507.
4. *Ibid.*, p. 509.

5. Louis Untermeyer, "E. A. R.: A Remembrance," *Saturday Review*, XLVIII (April 10, 1965), p. 34.
6. There is no reason to suppose that the subject of sex was taboo for Robinson in his associations with men and women, or that he remained forever fugitive from physical relations with women, a celibate both by preference and by practice. How he could have managed to support a wife, if he had taken one, say, before 1920, when he was fifty-one, is a matter that his more insensitive critics ignore. In any case, evidence in one unpublished letter reveals that Robinson was most assuredly not without some experience with women.
7. See Margaret Widdemer, *Summers at the Colony* (Syracuse, 1964).
8. Samuel A. Yorks, "Point of View in Two Poems," *University of Portland Review*, XVIII, 1 (Spring, 1966), 22-29.
9. Smith, *op. cit.*, pp. 181 ff.
10. Ellsworth Barnard remarks perceptively: ". . . in the long poem told in the third person there is sometimes a character set apart from the others by a temperament at once detached and sympathetic, whose often lengthy comments about his companions, made either to them or to others, may generally be taken at face value" (p. 174). He mentions Umfraville as one of these.
11. Indiana University Collection.
12. Mr. Barnard comments more extensively upon this increased usage in Robinson's later poems. See pp. 81-82.

Chapter Five

1. *SL*, p. 105.
2. Smith, *op. cit.*, p. 245.
3. *SL*, p. 113.
4. Letter to the present writer, July 1, 1930.
5. See, for example, Mr. Smith's study, pp. 110-13 and 230-35.
6. Frederic I. Carpenter, "Tristram the Transcendent," *New England Quarterly* (1938), XI, pp. 507-8.
7. Barnard, *op. cit.*, p. 85.
8. *Ibid.*, p. 86.
9. Smith, *op. cit.*, pp. 243-44.
10. *Ibid.*, p. 327.
11. *Ibid.*
12. *Ibid.*, p. 330. Mr. Smith develops an interesting thesis (pp. 323-30): "In terms of his beliefs with respect to the conflict between the outer self and its art and the inner self and its Grace or saintliness, Robinson's life divides into three periods. The first, running from his childhood till abut 1900, the completion of *Captain Craig*, was his Selfish Period. After a

transitional phase of a dozen years, the second, running from 1913 through 1923, the completion of *The Man Who Died Twice*, was his Gracious Period. The third, beginning in '27 and running to his death, was his Humanist Period." His "State of Grace" concept, equated with Robinson's "Light," "Love," or "Wisdom," Mr. Smith has drawn out of Puritan New England, particularly as it was engendered by Thomas Hooker, Thomas Shepard, and Jonathan Edwards. It is in this context that he discusses Isolt of Ireland, among other of Robinson's characters. The three periods seem to be somewhat arbitrary and the relationship of Robinson's symbols to the early Puritan theocrats rather nebulous and unconvincing. Just what took place in Robinson's thinking during the "transitional phase" needs clarification.

13. To Helen Grace Adams, January 1, 1930. *SL*, p. 160.
14. *SL*, p. 113.
15. *Ibid.*, p. 112.
16. *Ibid.*
17. *Ibid.*, p. 113.
18. Barnard, *op. cit.*, p. 104.
19. Coxe, *Edwin Arlington Robinson*, p. 41.

Chapter Six

1. Colby College Collection.
2. Yvor Winters, *Edwin Arlington Robinson*, (Norfolk, Conn., 1946), p. 39.
3. Louis O. Coxe, "E. A. Robinson: The Lost Tradition," *Sewanee Review*, LXII (1954), 247.
4. Neff, *op. cit.*, p. 263.
5. Barnard, *op. cit.*, p. 52.
6. Coxe, "E. A. Robinson: The Lost Tradition," pp. 247-66.
7. Coxe, *Edwin Arlington Robinson*, p. 45.
8. See Charles T. Davis, *Edwin Arlington Robinson: Selected Early Poems and Letters*, Intro., p. x. As Mr. Davis has pointed out, "Robinson's language from the beginning was prosy—not elegant or precious—and it offered the illusion of the colloquial. . . ."
9. See Edwin Fussell, *Edwin Arlington Robinson: The Literary Backgrounds of a Traditional Poet.* (Berkeley, 1954).
10. Mr. Smith's contention that "Robinson insisted on being a poet, on being simple, sensuous, and passionate," is difficult to accept without qualification. Simple, Robinson certainly intended to be. But that he is "sensuous, and passionate," that he appeals directly to the senses in his language, that he tends to rouse his readers to great heights of emotional response is

rarely the case. Some exceptions can of course be noted. Passages in *The Man Who Died Twice* and in *Tristram* are indeed sensuous and passionate. However, we do not discover everywhere in his work the same kind of emotional impact that we experience, for example, in Emily Dickinson's "I Heard a Fly Buzz. . . ." Perhaps the better term to use in Robinson's case is "intensity." The last line of "Richard Cory" is an instance of this intensity as is, it seems, the sestet in "Reuben Bright."

11. Floyd Stovall, "The Optimism Behind Robinson's Tragedies," *American Literature*, X (1938), 1-23.
12. Mr. Barnard, however, has analyzed many other aspects of Robinson's use of language.
13. See Neff, *op. cit.*, pp. 108-9.
14. Winters, *op. cit.*, p. 29.
15. Barnard, *op. cit.*, p. 189.
16. Smith, *Where the Light Falls*, p. 281.
17. Barnard, *op. cit.*, p. 208.
18. To Miss Bess Dworsky, *SL*, p. 166.
19. Coxe, *Edwin Arlington Robinson*, pp. 40-41.
20. Smith, *op. cit.*, p. 312.

Selected Bibliography

The Robinson bibliography is enormous. The following bibliography includes primary sources listed chronologically and, in secondary sources, only the most valuable and useful books that discuss Robinson and his poetry. Most, but by no means all, of the valuable periodical articles are listed in Notes and References.

PRIMARY SOURCES

A. *Poetry and Drama*

The Torrent and the Night Before. Privately printed. Cambridge, Mass.: The Riverside Press, 1896.

The Children of the Night. Boston: Richard G. Badger and Company, 1897.

Captain Craig. Boston and New York: Houghton, Mifflin and Company, 1902.

The Town Down the River: A Book of Poems. New York: Charles Scribner's Sons, 1910.

Van Zorn: A Comedy in Three Acts. New York: The Macmillan Company, 1914.

The Porcupine: A Drama in Three Acts. New York: The Macmillan Company, 1915.

The Man Against the Sky: A Book of Poems. New York: The Macmillan Company, 1916.

Merlin: A Poem. New York: The Macmillan Company, 1917.

Lancelot: A Poem. New York: Thomas Seltzer, 1920.

The Three Taverns: A Book of Poems. New York: The Macmillan Company, 1920.

Avon's Harvest. New York: The Macmillan Company, 1921.

Collected Poems. New York: The Macmillan Company, 1921.

Roman Bartholow. New York: The Macmillan Company, 1923.

The Man Who Died Twice. New York: The Macmillan Company, 1924.

Dionysus in Doubt: A Book of Poems. New York: The Macmillan Company, 1925.

Tristram. New York: The Macmillan Company, 1927.

Collected Poems. 5 vols. New York: The Macmillan Company, 1927.

Sonnets: 1889-1927. New York: The Macmillan Company, 1928.

Cavender's House. New York: The Macmillan Company, 1929.

Collected Poems. New York: The Macmillan Company, 1929.

The Glory of the Nightingales. New York: The Macmillan Company, 1930.

Selected Poems. With a Preface by BLISS PERRY. New York: The Macmillan Company, 1931.

Matthias at the Door. New York: The Macmillan Company, 1931.

Nicodemus: A Book of Poems. New York: The Macmillan Company, 1932.

Talifer. New York: The Macmillan Company, 1933.

Amaranth. New York: The Macmillan Company, 1934.

King Jasper. New York: The Macmillan Company, 1935. Published posthumously, with an introduction by Robert Frost.

In his *Selected Early Poems and Letters,* Charles T. Davis has made some important additions to the Robinson bibliography. (See pp. xxviii-xxix. New York: Holt, Rinehart and Winston, 1960.)

B.   *Letters*

Letters of Edwin Arlington Robinson to Howard G. Schmitt, ed. CARL J. WEBER. Waterville, Maine: Colby College Library, 1943.

Selected Letters of Edwin Arlington Robinson. Introduction by RIDGELY TORRENCE. New York: The Macmillan Company, 1940.

Untriangulated Stars: Letters of Edwin Arlington Robinson to Harry DeForest Smith, ed. DENHAM SUTCLIFFE. Cambridge, Mass.: Harvard University Press, 1947.

SECONDARY SOURCES

A.   *Bibliographies*

HOGAN, CHARLES BEECHER. *A Bibliography of Edwin Arlington Robinson.* New Haven: Yale University Press, 1936. Supplements issued.

LIPPINCOTT, LILLIAN. *A Bibliography of the Writing and Criticism of Edwin Arlington Robinson.* Boston: Faxton, 1937.

B.   *Books of Biography and Criticism*

ADLER, ELMER (ed.). *Breaking into Print.* New York: Simon and Schuster, 1937. Contains Robinson's account of his artistic apprenticeship, "The First Seven Years," reprinted from *The Colophon,* December, 1930.

BARNARD, ELLSWORTH. *Edwin Arlington Robinson: A Critical Study.* New York: The Macmillan Company, 1952. Most thorough, perceptive critical analysis of Robinson's poetry published to date. Carefully, usefully documented.

BROWN, ROLLO WALTER. *Next Door to a Poet.* New York: The Appleton-Century Company, 1937. Some interesting personal recollections of Robinson.

CESTRE, CHARLES. *Edwin Arlington Robinson.* New York: The Macmillan Company, 1930. Early critical monograph written by a most perceptive French scholar and teacher.

COXE, LOUIS. *E. A. Robinson.* Minneapolis: University of Minnesota Press, 1962. UMPAW, No. 17. Brief, useful survey of Robinson's poetic achievement.

DECKERT, PETER. *Edwin Arlington Robinson and Alanson Tucker Schumann: A Study in Influences.* Unpublished Doctoral dissertation, University of Pennsylvania, 1955. Only detailed study of the relationship between Robinson and the Gardiner poet-osteopath. Valuable information about Robinson's early efforts.

FUSSELL, EDWIN S. *Edwin Arlington Robinson: The Literary Background of a Traditional Poet.* Berkeley: University of California Press, 1954. Relates Robinson's poetry to known and probable sources. Emphasizes influence of Bible and Shakespeare but reveals the extent and diversity of Robinson's reading.

HAGEDORN, HERMANN. *Edwin Arlington Robinson.* New York: The Macmillan Company, 1938. The first extensive biography of the poet. Contains a large part of the known facts about the poet's life.

KAPLAN, ESTELLE. *Philosophy in the Poetry of Edwin Arlington Robinson.* New York: Columbia University Press, 1940. Extracts from Robinson's poetry the basic philosophical attitudes; reveals what most of Robinson's critics are agreed upon: Robinson not a systematic thinker, developed no integrated body of philosophy.

MASON, DANIEL GREGORY. *Music in My Time, and Other Reminiscences.* New York: The Macmillan Company, 1938. Reveals aspects of Robinson's personality.

NEFF, EMERY. *Edwin Arlington Robinson.* (American Men of Letters Series.) New York: Sloane Associates, 1948. A useful critical biography. Adds no new dimension to the biographical data, but critical judgments are often helpful.

SMITH, CHARD POWERS. *Where the Light Falls: A Portrait of Edwin Arlington Robinson.* New York: The Macmillan Company, 1965. First study to contain an extensive investigation of certain aspects of Robinson's personal history—the "legend." While some critics may question Mr. Smith's contentions regarding Robinson's philosophical and religious views, no one can doubt the thoroughness of his research.

WINTERS, YVOR. *Edwin Arlington Robinson.* Norfolk, Conn.: New Directions, 1946. Provocative, stimulating evaluation of Robinson's poetic achievement.

Index

Index